The Seven Great Monarchies of The Ancient Eastern World by George Rawlinson

Volume I (of VII) The First Monarchy: Chaldæa

George Rawlinson was born on 23rd November 1812 at Chadlington, Oxfordshire. He was the younger brother to the eminent Assyriologist, Sir Henry Rawlinson.

Rawlinson took his degree at Trinity College, Oxford in 1838. Here he also enjoyed playing cricket and was considered to have been a rare talent at the sport. In 1840 he was elected to a fellowship at Exeter College, Oxford. After being ordained in 1841 he became, from 1842 to 1846, a tutor there as well.

In 1846 Rawlinson married Louisa, the daughter of Sir RA Chermside.

His progress continued to be rapid and varied in acknowledgement of his undoubted talents. In 1859 he was made a Bampton lecturer, and was Camden Professor of Ancient History from 1861 to 1889.

By 1872 Rawlinson was appointed canon of Canterbury, and after 1888 he was rector of All Hallows, Lombard Street.

In 1873, he was made proctor in Convocation for the Chapter of Canterbury.

As a scholar he produced, either on his own or in collaboration, several works which are greatly thought of even to this day. His translation of the History of Herodotus (in collaboration with Sir Henry Rawlinson and Sir John Gardiner Wilkinson), 1858–60; The Five Great Monarchies of the Ancient Eastern World, 1862–67; which was later expanded to include The Sixth Great Oriental Monarchy (Parthian), 1873; and The Seventh Great Oriental Monarchy (Sassanian), 1875. Among his other works were Manual of Ancient History, 1869; Historical Illustrations of the Old Testament, 1871; The Origin of Nations, 1877; History of Ancient Egypt, 1881; Egypt and Babylon, 1885; History of Phoenicia, 1889; Parthia, 1893; Memoir of Major-General Sir HC Rawlinson, 1898.

His lectures to an audience at Oxford University on the topic of the accuracy of the Bible in 1859 were published as the apologetic work The Historical Evidences of the Truth of the Scripture Records Stated Anew in later years.

Despite this somewhat prodigious output and alongside his other clerical and family duties he contributed to the Speaker's Commentary, the Pulpit Commentary, Smith's Dictionary of the Bible, and various similar publications.

George Rawlinson died on 7th October, 1902 in Canterbury.

Index of Contents

List of Illustrations

MESOPOTAMIA, CHALDÆA, ASSYRIA and the adjacent Countries. Constructed from the latest Surveys.

PREFACE TO FIVE GREAT MONARCHIES

The history of Antiquity requires from time to time to be rewritten. Historical knowledge continually extends, in part from the advance of critical science, which teaches us little by little the true value of ancient authors, but also, and more especially, from the new discoveries which the enterprise of travellers and the patient toil of students are continually bringing to light, whereby the stock of our information as to the condition of the ancient world receives constant augmentation. The extremest scepticism cannot deny that recent researches in Mesopotamia and the adjacent countries have recovered a series of "monuments" belonging to very early times, capable of throwing considerable light on the Antiquities of the nations which produced them. The author of these volumes believes that, together with these remains, the languages of the ancient nations have been to a large extent recovered, and that a vast mass of written historical matter of a very high value is thereby added to the materials at the Historian's disposal. This is, clearly, not the place where so difficult and complicated a subject can be properly argued. The author is himself content with the judgment of "experts," and believes it would be as difficult to impose a fabricated language on Professor Lassen of Bonn and

Professor Max Miller of Oxford, as to palm off a fictitious for a real animal form on Professor Owen of London. The best linguists in Europe have accepted the decipherment of the cuneiform inscriptions as a thing actually accomplished. Until some good linguist, having carefully examined into the matter, declares himself of contrary opinion, the author cannot think that any serious doubt rests on the subject.

[Some writers allow that the Persian cuneiform inscriptions have been successfully deciphered and interpreted, but appear to doubt the interpretation of the Assyrian records. (See Edinburgh Review for July, 1862, Art Ill., p. 108.) Are they aware that the Persian inscriptions are accompanied in almost every instance by an Assyrian transcript, and that Assyrian interpretation thus follows upon Persian, without involving any additional "guess-work"]

The present volumes aim at accomplishing for the Five Nations of which they treat what Movers and Kenrick have accomplished for Phoenicia, or (still more exactly) what Wilkinson has accomplished for Ancient Egypt. Assuming the interpretation of the historical inscriptions as, in general, sufficiently ascertained, and the various ancient remains as assigned on sufficient grounds to certain peoples and epochs, they seek to unite with our previous knowledge of the five nations, whether derived from Biblical or classical sources, the new information obtained from modern discovery. They address themselves in a great measure to the eye; and it is hoped that even those who doubt the certainty of the linguistic discoveries in which the author believes, will admit the advantage of illustrating the life of the ancient peoples by representations of their productions. Unfortunately, the materials of this kind which recent explorations have brought to light are very unequally spread among the several nations of which it is proposed to treat, and even where they are most copious, fall short of the abundance of Egypt. Still in every case there is some illustration possible; and in one—Assyria—both the "Arts" and the "Manners" of the people admit of being illustrated very largely from the remains still extant.—[See Chapters VI. and VII. of the Second Monarchy]

The Author is bound to express his obligations to the following writers, from whose published works he has drawn freely: MM. Botta and Flandin, Mr. Layard, Mr. James Fergusson, Mr. Loftus, Mr. Cullimore, and Mr. Birch. He is glad to take this occasion of acknowledging himself also greatly beholden to the constant help of his brother, Sir Henry Rawlinson, and to the liberality of Mr. Faux, of the British Museum. The latter gentleman kindly placed at his disposal, for the purposes of the present work, the entire series of unpublished drawings made by the artists who accompanied Mr. Loftus in the last Mesopotamian Expedition, besides securing him undisturbed access to the Museum sculptures, thus enabling him to enrich the present volume with a large number of most interesting illustrations never previously given to the public. In the subjoined list these illustrations are carefully distinguished from such as, in one shape or another, have appeared previously.

Oxford, September, 1862.

In preparing for the press, after an interval of seven years, a second edition of this work, the author has found it unnecessary to make, excepting in two chapters, any important or exensive alterations. The exceptions are the chapters on the History and Chronology of Chaldaea and Assyria. So much fresh light has been thrown on these two subjects by additional discoveries, made partly by Sir Henry Rawlinson, partly by his assistant, Mr. George Smith, through the laborious study of fragmentary inscriptions now in the British Museum, that many pages of the two chapters in question required to be written afresh, and the Chronological Schemes required, in the one case a complete, and in the other a partial, revision. In making this revision, both of the Chronology and the History, the author has received the most valuable assistance both from the published papers and from the private communications of Mr. Smith—an assistance for which he desires to make in this place the warmest and most hearty acknowledgment. He is also beholden to a recent Eastern traveller, Mr. A. D. Berrington, for some valuable notes on the physical geography and productions of Mesopotamia, which have been embodied in the accounts given of those subjects. A few corrections have likewise been made of errors pointed out by anonymous critics. Substantially, however, the work continues such as it was on its first appearance, the author having found that time only deepened his conviction of the reality of cuneiform decipherment, and of the authenticity of the history obtained by means of it.

OXFORD, November, 1870.

CHAPTER I

GENERAL VIEW OF THE COUNTRY

"Behold the land of the Chaldaeans."—ISAIAH xxiii. 13.

The broad belt of desert which traverses the eastern hemisphere, in a general direction from west to east (or, speaking more exactly, of W. S. W. to N. E. E.), reaching from the Atlantic on the one hand nearly to the Yellow Sea on the other, is interrupted about its centre by a strip of rich vegetation, which at once breaks the continuity of the arid region, and serves also to mark the point where the desert changes its character from that of a plain at a low level to that of an elevated plateau or table-land. West of the favored district, the Arabian and African wastes are seas of sand, seldom raised much above, often sinking below, the level of the ocean; while east of the same, in Persia, Kerman, Seistan, Chinese Tartary, and Mongolia, the desert consists of a series of plateaus, having from 3000 to nearly 10,000 feet of elevation. The green and fertile region, which is thus interposed between the "highland" and the "lowland" deserts, participates, curiously enough, in both characters. Where the belt of sand is intersected by the valley of the Nile, no marked change of elevation occurs; and the continuous low desert is merely interrupted by a few miles of green and cultivable surface, the whole of which is just as smooth and as flat as the waste on either side of it. But it is otherwise at the more eastern interruption. There the verdant and productive country divides itself into two tracts, running parallel to each other, of which the western presents features not unlike those that characterize the Nile valley, but on a far larger scale; while the eastern is a lofty mountain region, consisting for the most part of five or six parallel ranges, and mounting in many places far above the level of perpetual snow.

It is with the western or plain tract that we are here concerned. Between the outer limits of the Syro-Arabian desert and the foot of the great mountain range of Kurdistan and Luristan intervenes a territory long famous in the world's history, and the chief site of three out of the five empires of whose history, geography, and antiquities it is proposed to treat in the present volumes. Known to the Jews as Aram-Naharaim, or "Syria of the two rivers;" to the Greeks and Romans as Mesopotamia, or "the between-river country;" to the Arabs as Al-Jezireh, or "the island," this district has always taken its name from the streams, which constitute its most striking feature, and to which, in fact, it owes its existence. If it were not for the two great rivers—the Tigris and Euphrates—with their tributaries, the more northern part of the Mesopotamian lowland would in no respect differ from the Syro-Arabian desert on which it adjoins, and which in latitude, elevation, and general geological character it exactly resembles. Towards the south, the importance of the rivers is still greater; for of Lower Mesopotamia it may be said, with more truth than of Egypt, that it is "an acquired land," the actual "gift" of the two streams which wash it on either side; being, as it is, entirely a recent formation—a deposit which the streams have made in the shallow waters of a gulf into which they have flowed for many ages.

The division, which has here forced itself upon our notice, between the Upper and the Lower Mesopotamian country, is one very necessary to engage our attention in connection with the ancient Chaldaea. There is no reason to think that the terns Chaldaea had at anytime the extensive signification of Mesopotamia, much less that it applied to the entire flat country between the desert and the mountains. Chaldaea was not the whole, but a part of, the great Mesopotamian plain; which was ample enough to contain within it three or four considerable monarchies. According to the combined testimony of geographers and historians, Chaldaea lay towards the south, for it bordered upon the Persian Gulf; and towards the west, for it adjoined Arabia. If we are called upon to fix more accurately its boundaries, which, like those of most countries without strong natural frontiers, suffered many fluctuations, we are perhaps entitled to say that the Persian Gulf on the south, the Tigris on the east, the Arabian desert on the west, and the limit between Upper and Lower Mesopotamia on the north, formed the natural bounds, which were never greatly exceeded and never much infringed upon. These boundaries are for the most part tolerably clear, though the northern only is invariable. Natural causes, hereafter to be mentioned more particularly, are perpetually varying the course of the Tigris, the shore of the Persian Gulf, and the line of demarcation between the sands of Arabia and the verdure of the Euphrates valley. But nature has set a permanent mark, half way down the Mesopotamian lowland, by a difference of geological structure, which is very conspicuous. Near Hit on the Euphrates, and a little below Samarah on the Tigris, the traveller who descends the streams, bids adieu to a somewhat waving and slightly elevated plain of secondary formation, and enters on the dead flat and low level of the mere alluvium. The line thus formed is marked and invariable; it constitutes the only natural division between the upper and lower portions of the valley; and both probability and history point to it as the actual boundary between Chaldaea and her northern neighbor.

The extent of ancient Chaldaea is, even after we have fixed its boundaries, a question of some difficulty. From the edge of the alluvium a little below Hit, to the present coast of the Persian Gulf at the mouth of the Shat-el-Arab, is a distance of above 430 miles; while from the western shore of the Bahr-i-Nedjif to the Tigris at Serut is a direct distance of 185 miles. The present area of the alluvium west of the Tigris and the Shat-el-Arab maybe estimated at about 30,000 square miles. But the extent of ancient Chaldaea can scarcely have been so great. It is certain that the alluvium at the head of the Persian Gulf now grows with extraordinary rapidity, and not improbable that the growth may in ancient times have been even more rapid than it is at present. Accurate observations have shown that the present rate of increase amounts to as much as a mile each seventy years, while it is the opinion of those best qualified to judge that the average progress during the historic period has been as much as a mile in every thirty years! Traces of post-tertiary deposits have been found as far up the country as Tel Ede and Hammam, 10 or more than 200 miles from the embouchure of the Shat-el-Arab; and there is ample reason for believing that at the time when the first Chaldaean monarchy was established, the Persian Gulf reached inland, 120 or 130 miles further than at present. We must deduct therefore from the estimate of extent grounded upon the existing state of things, a tract of land 130 miles long and some 60 or 70 broad, which has been gained from the sea in the course of about forty centuries. This deduction will reduce Chaldaea to a kingdom of somewhat narrow limits; for it will contain no more than about 23,000 square miles. This, it is true, exceeds the area of all ancient Greece, including Thessaly, Acarnania, and the islands; it nearly equals that of the Low Countries, to which Chaldaea presents some analogy; it is almost exactly that of the modern kingdom of Denmark; but it is less than Scotland, or Ireland, or Portugal, or Bavaria; it is more than doubled by England, more than quadrupled by Prussia, and more than octupled by Spain, France, and European Turkey. Certainly, therefore, it was not in consequence of its size that Chaldaea became so important a country in the early ages, but rather in consequence of certain advantages of the soil, climate, and position, which will be considered in the next chapter.

It has been already noticed that in the ancient Chaldaea, the chief—almost the sole-geographical features, were the rivers. Nothing is more remarkable even now than the featureless character of the region, although in the course of ages it has received from man some interruptions of the original uniformity. On all sides a dead level extends itself, broken only by single solitary mounds, the remains of ancient temples or cities, by long lines of slightly elevated embankment marking the course of canals, ancient or recent, and towards the south—by a few sand-hills. The only further variety is that of color; for while the banks of the streams, the marsh-grounds, and the country for a short distance on each side of the canals in actual operation, present to the eye a pleasing, and in some cases a luxuriant verdure; the rest, except in early spring, is parched and arid, having little to distinguish it from the most desolate districts of Arabia. Anciently, except for this difference, the tract must have possessed all the wearisome uniformity of the steppe region; the level horizon must have shown itself on all sides unbroken by a single irregularity; all places must have appeared alike, and the traveller can scarcely have perceived his progress, or have known whither or how to direct his steps. The rivers alone, with their broad sweeps and bold reaches, their periodical changes of swell and fall, their strength, motion, and life-giving power, can have been objects of thought and interest to the first inhabitants; and it is still to these that the modern must turn who wishes to represent, to himself or others, the general aspect and chief geographical divisions of the country.

The Tigris and Euphrates rise from opposite sides of the same mountain-chain. This is the ancient range of Niphates (a prolongation of Taurus), the loftiest of the many parallel ridges which intervene between the Euxine and the Mesopotamian plain, and the only one which transcends in many places the limits of perpetual snow. Hence its ancient appellation, and hence its power to sustain unfailingly the two magnificent streams which flow from it. The line of the Niphates is from east to west, with a very slight deflection to the south of west; and the streams thrown off from its opposite flanks, run at first in valleys parallel to the chain itself, but in opposite directions, the Euphrates flowing westward from its source near Ararat to Malatiyeh, while the Tigris from Diarbekr "goes eastward to Assyria." The rivers thus appear as if never about to meet; but at Malatiyeh, the course of the Euphrates is changed. Sweeping suddenly to the south-east, this stream passes within a few miles of the source of the Tigris below Lake Goljik, and forces a way through the mountains towards the south, pursuing a tortuous course, but still seeming as if it intended ultimately to mingle its waters with those of the Mediterranean. It is not till about Balis, in lat. 36 deg., that this intention appears to be finally relinquished, and the convergence of the two streams begins. The Euphrates at first flows nearly due east, but soon takes a course which is, with few and unimportant deflections, about south-east, as far as Suk-es-Sheioukh, after which it runs a little north of east to Kurnah. The Tigris from Til to Mosul pursues also a south-easterly course, and draws but a very little nearer to the Euphrates. From Mosul, however, to Samarah, its course is only a point east of south; and though, after that, for some miles it flows off to the east, yet resuming, a little below the thirty-fourth parallel, its southerly direction, it is brought about Baghdad within twenty miles of the sister stream. From this point there is again a divergence. The course of the Euphrates, which from Hit to the mounds of Mohammed (long. 44 deg.) had been E.S.E., becomes much more southerly, while that of the Tigris—which, as we have seen, was for awhile due south—becomes once more only slightly south of east, till near Serut, where the distance between the rivers has increased from twenty to a hundred miles. After passing respectively Serut and El Khitr, the two streams converge rapidly. The flow of the Euphrates is at first E. S. E., and then a little north of east to Kurnah, while that of the Tigris is S.S.E. to the same point. The lines of the streams in this last portion of their course, together with that which may be drawn across from stream to stream, form nearly an equilateral triangle, the distance being respectively 104, 110, and 115 miles. So rapid is the final convergence of the two great rivers.

The Tigris and Euphrates are both streams of the first order. The estimated length of the former, including main windings, is 1146 miles; that of the latter is 1780 miles. Like most rivers that have their sources in high mountain regions, they are strong from the first, and, receiving in their early course a vast number of important tributaries, become broad and deep streams before they issue upon the plains. The Euphrates is navigable from Sumeisat (the ancient Samosata), 1200 miles above its embouchure; and even 180 miles higher up, is a river "of imposing appearance," 120 yards wide and very deep. The Tigris is often 250 yards wide at Diarbekr, which is not a hundred miles from its source, and is navigable in the flood time from the bridge of Diarbekr to Mosul, from which place it is descended at all seasons to Baghdad, and thence to the sea. Its average width below Mosul is 200 yards, with a depth which allows the ascent of light steamers, unless when there is an artificial obstruction. Above Mosul the width rarely exceeds 150 yards, and the depth is not more in places than three or four feet. The Euphrates is 250 yards wide at Balbi, and averages 350 yards from its junction with the Khabour to Hit: its depth is commonly from fifteen to twenty feet. Small steamers have descended its entire course from Bir to the sea. The volume of the Euphrates in places is, however, somewhat less than that of the Tigris, which is a swifter and in its latter course a deeper stream. It has been calculated that the quantity of water discharged every second by the Tigris at Baghdad is 164,103 cubic feet, while that discharged by the Euphrates at Hit is 72,804 feet.

The Tigris and Euphrates are very differently circumstanced with respect to tributaries. So long as it runs among the Armenian mountains, the Euphrates has indeed no lack of affluents; but these, except the Kara Su, or northern Euphrates, are streams of no great volume, being chiefly mountain-torrents which collect the drainage of very limited basins. After it leaves the mountains and enters upon a low country at Sumefsat, the affluents almost entirely cease; one, the river of Sajur, is received from the right, in about lat. 36 deg. 40'; and two of more importance flow in from the left-the Belik (ancient Bilichus), which joins it in long. 39 deg. 9'; and the Khabour (ancient Habor or Chaboras), which effects a junction in long. 40 deg. 30', lat. 35 deg. 7'. The Belik and Khabour collect the waters which flow from the southern flank of the mountain range above Orfa, Mardin, and Nisibin, best known as the "Mons Masius" of Strabo. They are not, however, streams of equal importance. The Belik has a course which is nearly straight, and does not much exceed 120 miles. The Khabour, on the contrary, is sufficiently sinuous, and its course may be reckoned at fully 200 miles. It is navigable by rafts from the junction of its two main branches near the volcanic cone of Koukab, and adds a considerable body of water to the Euphrates. Below its confluence with this stream, or during the last 800 miles of its course, the Euphrates does not receive a single tributary. On the contrary, it soon begins to give off its waters right and left, throwing out branches, which either terminate in marshes, or else empty themselves into the Tigris. After awhile, indeed, it receives compensation, by means of the Shat-el-Hie and other branch streams, which bring back to it from the Tigris, between Mugheir and Kurnah, the greater portion of the borrowed fluid. The Tigris, on the contrary, is largely enriched throughout the whole of its course by the waters of tributary streams. It is formed originally of three main branches: the Diarbekr stream, or true Tigris, the Myafarekin River, and the Bitlis Chai, or Centrites of Xenophon, which carries a greater body than either of the other two. From its entry on the low country near Jezireh to the termination of its course at Kurnah, it is continually receiving from the left a series of most important additions. The chain of Zagros, which, running parallel to the two main springs, shuts in the Mesopotamian plain upon the east, abounds with springs, which are well supplied during the whole summer from its snows, and these when collected form rivers of large size and most refreshing coolness. The principal are, the eastern Khabour, which joins the Tigris in lat. 37 deg. 12': the Upper Zabo which falls in by the ruins of Nimrud: the Lower Zab, which joins some way below Kileh Sherghat: the Adhem, which unites its waters half way between Samarah and Baghdad: and the Diyaleh (ancient Gyndes), which is received between Baghdad and the ruins of Ctesiphon.

By the influx of these streams the Tigris continues to grow in depth and strength as it nears the sea, and becomes at last (as we have seen) a greater river than the Euphrates, which shrinks during the latter part of its course, and is reduced to a volume very inferior to that which it once boasted. The Euphrates at its junction with the Khabour, 700 miles above Kurnah, is 400 yards wide and 18 feet deep; at Irzah or Verdi, 75 miles lower down, it is 350 yards wide and of the same depth; at Hadiseh, 140 miles below Werdi, it is 300 yards wide, and still of the same depth; at Hit, 50 miles below Hadiseh, its width has increased to 350 yards, but its depth has diminished to 16 feet; at Felujiah, 75 miles from Hit, the depth is 20 feet, but the width has diminished to 250 yards. From this point the contraction is very rapid and striking. The Saklawiyeh canal is given out upon the left, and some way further down the Hindiyeh branches off upon the right, each carrying, when the Euphrates is full, a large body of water. The consequence is that at Hillah, 90 miles-below Felujiah, the stream is no more than 200 yards wide and 15 feet deep; at Diwaniyeh, 65 miles further down, it is only 160 yards wide; and at Lamlun, 20 miles below Diwaniyeh, it is reduced to 120 yards wide, with a depth of no more than 12 feet! Soon after, however, it begins to recover itself. The water, which left it by the Hindiyeh, returns to it upon the one side, while the Shat-el-Hie and numerous other branch streams from the Tigris flow in upon the other; but still the Euphrates never recovers itself entirely, nor even approaches in its later course to the standard of its earlier greatness. The channel from Kurnah to El Khitr was found by Colonel Chesney to have an average width of only 200 yards, and a depth of about 18 or 19 feet, which implies a body of water far inferior to that carried between the junction with the Khabour and Hit. More recently, the decline of the stream in its latter course has been found to be even greater. Neglect of the banks has allowed the river to spread itself more and more widely over the land: and it is said that, except in the flood time, very little of the Euphrates water reaches the sea. Nor is this an unprecedented or very unusual state of things. From the circumstance (probably) that it has been formed by the deposits of streams flowing from the east as well as from the north, the lower Mesopotamian plain slopes not only to the south, but to the west. The Euphrates, which has low banks, is hence at all times inclined to leave its bed, and to flow off to the right, where large tracts are below its ordinary level. Over these it spreads itself, forming the well-known "Chaldaean marshes," which absorb the chief proportion of the water that flows into them, and in which the "great river" seems at various times to have wholly, or almost wholly, lost itself. No such misfortune can befall the Tigris, which runs in a deep bed, and seldom varies its channel, offering a strong contrast to the sister stream.

Frequent allusion has been made, in the course of this description of the Tigris and Euphrates, to the fact of their having each a flood season. Herodotus is scarcely correct when he says that in Babylonia "the river does not, as in Egypt, overflow the corn-lands of its own accord, but is spread over them by the help of engines." Both the Tigris and Euphrates rise many feet each spring, and overflow their banks in various places. The rise is caused by the melting of the snows in the mountain regions from which the two rivers and their affluents spring. As the Tigris drains the southern, and the Euphrates the northern side of the same mountain range, the flood of the former stream is earlier and briefer than that of the latter. The Tigris commonly begins to rise early in March, and reaches its greatest height in the first or second week of May, after which it rapidly declines, and returns to its natural level by the middle of June. The Euphrates first swells about the middle of March, and is not in full flood till quite the end of May or the beginning of June; it then continues high for above a month, and does not sink much till the middle of July, after which it gradually falls till September. The country inundated by the Tigris is chiefly that on its lower course, between the 32d and 31st parallels, the territory of the Beni Lam Arabs. The territory which the Euphrates floods is far more extensive. As high up as its junction with the Khabour, that stream is described as, in the month of April, "spreading over the surrounding country like a sea." From Hit downwards, it inundates both its banks, more especially the country above Baghdad (to which it is carried by the Saklawiyeh canal), the tract west of the Birs Nimrud and extending thence by way of Nedjif to Samava and the territory of the Affej Arabs, between the rivers above and below the 32d parallel. Its flood is, however, very irregular, owing to the nature of its banks, and the general inclination of the plain, whereof mention was made above. If care is taken, the inundation may be pretty equally distrib uted on either side of the stream; but if the river banks are neglected, it is sure to flow mainly to the west, rendering the whole country on that side the river a swamp, and leaving the territory on the left bank almost without water. This state of things may be traced historically from the age of Alexander to the present day, and has probably prevailed more or less since the time when Chaldaea received its first inhabitants.

The floods of the Tigris and Euphrates combine with the ordinary action of their streams upon their banks to produce a constant variation in their courses, which in a long period of time might amount to something very considerable. It is impossible to say, with respect to any portion of the alluvial plain, that it may not at some former period have been the bed of one or the other river. Still it would seem that, on the whole, a law of compensation prevails, with the result that the general position of the streams in the valley is not very different now from what it was 4000 years ago. Certainly between the present condition of things and that in the time of Alexander, or even of Herodotus, no great difference can be pointed out, except in the region immediately adjoining on the gulf, where the alluvium has grown, and the streams, which were formerly separate, have united their waters. The Euphrates still flows by Hit and through Babylon; the Tigris passes near Opis, and at Baghdad runs at the foot of an embankment made to confine it by Nebuchadnezzar. The changes traceable are less in the main courses than in the branch streams, which perpetually vary, being sometimes left dry within a few years of the time that they have been navigable channels.

The most important variations of this kind are on the side of Arabia. Here the desert is always ready to encroach; and the limits of Chaldaea itself depend upon the distance from the main river, to which some branch stream conveys the Euphrates water. In the most flourishing times of the country, a wide and deep channel, branching off near Hit, at the very commencement of the alluvium, has skirted the Arabian rock and gravel for a distance of several hundred miles, and has entered the Persian Gulf by a mouth of its own. In this way the extent of Chaldaea has been at times largely increased, a vast tract being rendered cultivable, which is otherwise either swamp or desert.

Such are the chief points of interest connected with the two great Mesopotamian rivers. These form, as has been already observed, the only marked and striking characteristics of the country, which, except for them, and for one further feature, which now requires notice, would be absolutely unvaried and uniform. On the Arabian side of the Euphrates, 50 miles south of the ruins of Babylon, and 25 or 30 miles from the river, is a fresh-water lake of very considerable dimensions—the Bahr-i-Nedjif, the "Assyrium stagnum" of Justin. This is a natural basin, 40 miles long, and from 10 to 20 miles broad, enclosed on three sides by sandstone cliffs, varying from 20 to 200 feet in height, and shut in on the fourth side—the north-east—by a rocky ridge, which intervenes between the valley of the Euphrates and this inland sea. The cliffs are water-worn, presenting distinct indications of more than one level at which the water has rested in former times. At the season of the inundation this lake is liable to be confounded with the extensive floods and marshes which extend continuously from the country west of the Birs Nimrud to Samava. But at other tines the distinction between the Bahr and the marshes is very evident, the former remaining when the latter disappear altogether, and not diminishing very greatly in size even in the driest season. The water of the lake is fresh and sweet, so long as it communicates with the Euphrates; when the communication is cut off it becomes very unpalatable, and those who dwell in the vicinity are no longer able to drink it. This result is attributed to the connection of the lake with rocks of the gypsiferous series.

It is obvious that the only natural divisions of Chaldaea a proper are those made by the river-courses. The principal tract must always have been that which intervenes between the two streams. This was anciently a district some 300 miles in length, varying from 20 to 100 miles in breadth, and perhaps averaging 50 miles, which must thus have contained an area of about 15,000 square miles. The tract between the Euphrates and Arabia was at all times smaller than this, and in the most flourishing period of Chaldaea must have fallen short of 10,000 square miles.

We have no evidence that the natural division of Chaldaea here indicated was ever employed in ancient times for political purposes. The division which appears to have been so employed was one into northern and southern Chaldaea, the first extending from Hit to a little below Babylon, the second from Niffer to the shores of the Persian Gulf. In each of these districts we have a sort of tetrarchy, or special pre-eminence of four cities, such as appears to be indicated by the words—"The beginning of his kingdom was Babel, and Erech, and Accad and Calneh, in the land of Shinar." The southern tetrarchy is composed of the four cities, Ur or Hur, Huruk, Nipur, and Larsa or Larancha, which are probably identified with the Scriptural "Ur of the Chaldees," Erech, Calneh, and Ellasar. The northern consists of Babel or Babylon, Borsippa, Cutha, and Sippara, of which all except Borsippa are mentioned in Scripture. Besides these cities the country contained many others,—as Chilmad, Dur-Kurri-galzu, Ihi or Ahava, Rubesi, Duran, Tel-Humba, etc. It is not possible at present to locate with accuracy all these places. We may, however, in the more important instances, fix either certainly, or with a very high degree of probability, their position.

Hur or Ur, the most important of the early capitals, was situated on the Euphrates, probably at no great distance from its mouth. It was probably the chief commercial emporium in the early times; as in the bilingual vocabularies its ships are mentioned in connection with those of Ethiopia. The name is found to have attached to the extensive ruins (now about six miles from the river, on its right bank, and nearly opposite its junction with the Shat-el-Hie) which are known by the name of Mugheir, or "the bitumened." Hereon a dead flat, broken only by a few sand-hills, are traces of a considerable town, consisting chiefly of a series of low mounds, disposed in an oval shape, the largest diameter of which runs from north to south, and measures somewhat more than half a mile. The chief building is a temple, hereafter to be more particularly described, which is a very conspicuous object even at a considerable distance, its greatest height above the plain being about seventy feet. It is built in a very rude fashion, of large bricks, cemented with bitumen, whence the name by which the Arabs designate the ruins.

About thirty miles from Hur, in a north-westerly direction, and on the other side of the Euphrates, from which it is distant eight or nine miles, are the ruins of a town, called in the inscriptions Larrak, or Larsa, in which some of the best Orientalists have recognized at once the Biblical Ellasar, the Laranchue of Berosus, and the Larissa of Apollodorus, where the king held his court who sent Memnon to the siege of Troy. The identification is perhaps doubtful; but, at any rate, we have here the remains of a second

Chaldaean capital, dating from the very earliest times. The ruins, which bear now the name of Senkereh or Sinkara, consist of a low circular platform, about four and a half miles in circumference, rising gradually from the level of the plain to a central mound, the highest point of which attains an elevation of seventy feet above the plain itself, and is distinctly visible from a distance of fifteen miles. The material used consists of the ordinary sun-dried and baked bricks; and the basement platforms bear the inscriptions of the same king who appears to have been the original founder of the chief buildings at Ur or Mugheir.

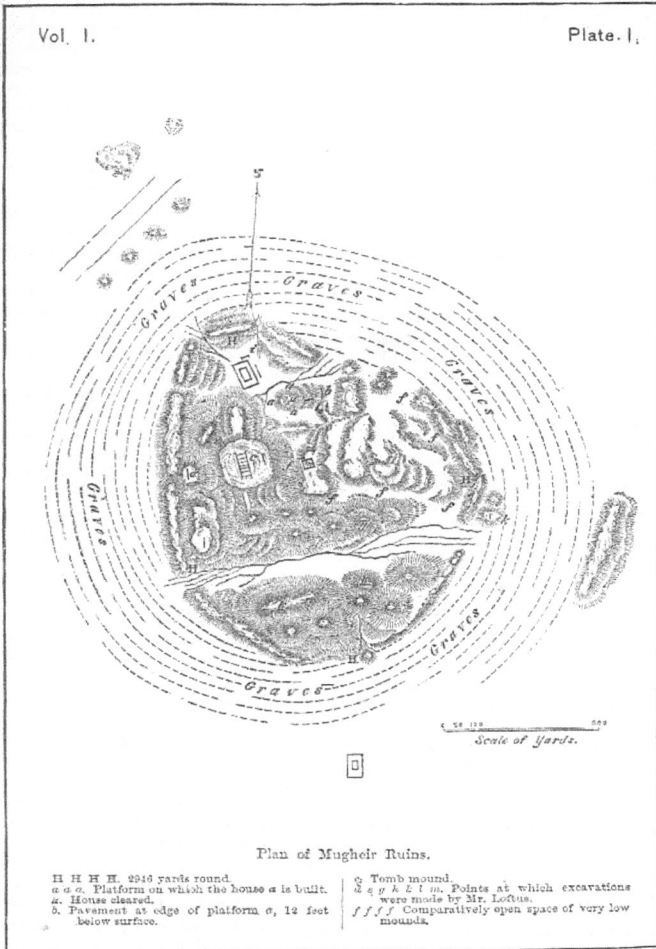

Vol. I.   Plate. I.

Plan of Mugheir Ruins.

H H H H, 2946 yards round.
a a a, Platform on which the house a is built.
a, House cleared.
b, Pavement at edge of platform a, 12 feet below surface.

c, Tomb mound.
d e g h k l m, Points at which excavations were made by Mr. Loftus.
f f f f, Comparatively open space of very low mounds.

Scale of Yards.

PLATE I

Plate II.

Vol. I.

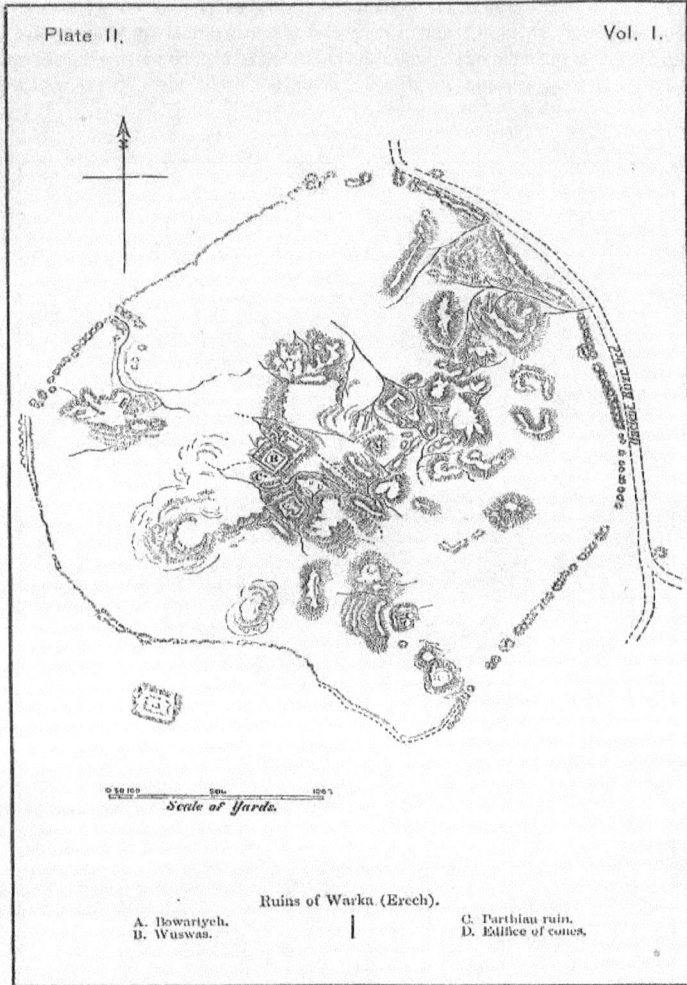

Ruins of Warka. (Erech).

A. Bowariyeh.
B. Wuswas.

C. Parthian ruin.
D. Edifice of cones.

Scale of Yards.

PLATE II

Fifteen miles from Larsa, in a direction a little north of west, and on the same side of the river, are ruins considerably more extensive than those of either Ur or Larsa, to which the natives apply the name of Warka, which is no doubt a corruption of the original appellation. The Erech, or Orech, of the Hebrews, which appears as Huruk in the cuneiform geographical lists, became known to the Greeks as Orchoe;

and this appellation, probably continuing in use to the time of the Arab conquest, was then corrupted into Urka or Warka, in which shape the name given by Nimrod still attaches to the second of his cities. The ruins stand in lat. 31 deg. 19', long. 45 deg. 40', about four miles from the nearest bend of the Euphrates, on its left or east bank. They form an irregular circle, nearly six miles in circumference, which is defined by the traces of an earthen rampart, in some places forty feet high. A vast mass of undulating mounds, intersected by innumerable channels and ravines, extends almost entirely across the circular space, in a direction, which is nearly north and south, abutting at either end upon the rampart. East and west of this mass is a comparatively open space, where the mounds are scattered and infrequent; while outside the rampart are not only a number of detached hillocks marking the site of ancient buildings, but in one direction—towards the east—the city may be traced continuously by means of ruined edifices, mounds, and pottery, fully three miles beyond the rampart into the desert. The greatest height of the ruins is about 100 feet; their construction is very rude and primitive, the date of some buildings being evidently as early as that of the most ancient structures of either Mugheir or Senkereh.

Sixty miles to the north-west of these ruins, still on the left or eastern bank of the Euphrates, but at the distance of thirty miles from its present course, are the remains of another city, the only Chaldaean ruins which can dispute, with those already described, the palm of antiquity. They consist of a number of separate and distinct heaps, which seem to be the remains of different buildings, and are divided into two nearly equal groups by a deep ravine or channel 120 feet wide, apparently the dry bed of a river which once ran through the town. Conspicuous among the other hillocks is a conical heap, occupying a central position on the eastern side of the river-bed, and rising to the height of about seventy feet above the general level of the plain. Further on in this direction is a low continuous mound, which seems to be a portion of the outer wall of the city. The ruins are of considerable extent, but scarcely so large as those at either Senkereh or Warka. The name which now attaches to them is Niffer: and it appears, from the inscriptions at the place, that the ancient Semitic appellation was but slightly different. This name, as read on the bilingual tablets, was Nipur; and as there can be little doubt that it is this word which appears in the Talmud as Nopher, we are perhaps entitled, on the authority of that treasure-house of Hebrew traditions, to identify these ruins with the Calneh of Moses, and the Calno of Isaiah.

About sixty-five miles from Niffer, on the opposite side of the Euphrates, and in a direction only slightly north of west, are the remains of the ancient Borsippa. These consist of little more than the ruins of a single building—the great temple of Merodach—which was entirely rebuilt by Nebuchadnezzar. They have been sometimes regarded as really a portion of the ancient Babylon; but this view is wholly incompatible with the cuneiform records, which distinctly assign to the ruins in question the name of Borsip or Borsippa, a place known with certainty to have been distinct from, though in the neighborhood of, the capital. A remnant of the ancient name appears to be contained in the modern appellation, Birs-Nimrud or Birsi-Nimrud, which does not admit of any explanation from the existing language of the country.

Fifteen miles from thence, to the north-east, chiefly but not entirely on the left or east bank of the Euphrates, are the remains of "Babylon the Great," which have been so frequently described by travellers, that little need be said of them in this place. The chief ruins cover a space about three miles long, and from one to two broad, and consist mainly of three great masses: the first a square mound, called "Babil" by the Arabs, lying towards the north at some distance from the other remains; the second or central mound, a pile called the "Kasr" or Palace; and the third, a great irregular heap lying towards the south, known as the "mound of Amram," from a tomb which crowns its summit. The "Kasr" and "Amram" mounds are enclosed within two lines of rampart, lying at right angles to each other, and forming, with the river, a sort of triangle, within which all the principal ruins are comprised, except the mound called "Babil". Beyond the rampart, towards the north, south, and east, and also across the river to the west, are various smaller detached ruins, while the whole ground, in every direction, is covered with fragments of brick and with nitre, the sure marks of former habitations.

Vol. 1.

Plate III

Fig. 1.

Akkerkuf.

Fig. 2.

Hammam.

PLATE III

The other cities of ancient Chaldaea which may be located with an approach to certainty, are Cutha, now Ibrahim, fifteen miles north-east by north of Hymar; Sippara or Sepharvaim, which was at Sura, near Mosaib on the Euphrates, about twenty miles above Babylon by the direct route; and Dur-Kurri-galzu, now Akkerkuf, on the Saklawiyeh canal, six miles from Baghdad, and thirty from Mosaib, in a direction a little west of north. [PLATE III., Fig. 1.] Ihi, or Ahava, is probably Hit, ninety miles above Mosaib, on the right bank of the river; Chilmad may be Kalwadha, near Baghdad; and Rubesi is perhaps Zerghul, near the left bank of the Shat-el-Hie, a little above its confluence with the Euphrates. Chaldaean cities appear likewise to have existed at Hymar, ten miles from Babylon towards the east; at Sherifeh and Im Khithr, south and south-east of Hymar; at Zibbliyeh, on the line of the Nil canal, fifteen miles north-west of Niffer; at Delayhim and Bisrniya, in the Affej marshes, beyond Niffer, to the south-east; at Phara and Jidr, in the same region, to the south-west and south-east of Bismiya; at Hammam [PLATE III., Fig. 2], sixteen miles south-east of Phara, between the Affej and the Shatra marshes; at Tel-Ede, six miles from Hammam, to the south-south-west [PLATE IV., Fig. 2]; at Tel-Medineh and Tel-Sifr, in the Shatra marshes, to the south-east of Tel-Ede and the north-east of Senkereh; at Yokha, east of Hammam, and Nuffdyji, north of Warka; at Lethami, near Niffer; at Iskhuriyeh, north of Zibbliyeh, near the Tigris; at Tel-Kheir and Tel-Dhalab, in the upper part of the alluvium, to the north of Akkerkuf; at Duair, on the right bank of the Euphrates, south of Hilleh and south-east of the Birs-Nimrud; at Jeb Mehari, south of the Bahr-i-Nedjif; at Mal Battush, near Swaje; at Tel-el-Lahm, nine or ten miles south of Suk-es-Sheioukh, and at Abu Shahrein, in the same neighborhood, on the very border of the Arabian Desert. Further investigation will probably add largely to this catalogue, for many parts of Babylonia are still to some extent unexplored. This is especially true of the tract between the Shat-el-Hie and the lower Tigris, a district which, according to the geographers, abounds with ruins.

PLATE IV

No doubt the most extensive and most striking of the old cities have been visited; for of these Europeans are sure to hear through the reports of natives. But it is more than probable that a number of the most interesting sites remain unexplored, and even unvisited; for these are not always either very extensive or very conspicuous. The process of gradual disintegration is continually lowering the height of the Chaldaean ruins; and depressed mounds are commonly the sign of an ancient and long-deserted city. Such remains give us an insight into the character of the early people, which it is impossible to obtain from ruins where various populations have raised their fabrics in succession upon the same spot.

The cities here enumerated may not perhaps, in all cases, have existed in the Chaldaean period. The evidence hitherto obtained connects distinctly with that period only the following—Babylon, Ur or Hur, Larrak or Larsa, Erech or Huruk, Calneh or Nopher, Sippara, Dur-Kurri-galzu, Chilmad, and the places now called Abu Shahrein and Tel-Sifr. These sites, it will be observed, were scattered over the whole territory from the extreme south almost to the extreme north, and show the extent of the kingdom to have been that above assigned to it. They are connected together by a similarity in building arrangements and materials, in language, in form of type and writing, and sometimes in actual names of monarchs. The most ancient, apparently, are those towards the south, at Warka, Senkereh, Mugheir, and Niffer; and here, in the neighborhood of the sea, which then probably reached inland as far as Suk-es-Sheioukh, there is sufficient reason to place the primitive seat of Chaldaean power. The capital of the whole region was at first Ur or Hur, but afterwards became Nipur, and finally Babel or Babylon.

The geography of Chaldaea is scarcely complete without a glance at the countries which adjoin upon it. On the west, approaching generally within twenty or thirty miles of the present course of the Euphrates, is the Arabian Desert, consisting in this place of tertiary sand and gravels, having a general elevation of a few feet above the Mesopotamian plain, and occasionally rising into ridges of no great height, whose direction is parallel to the course of the great stream. Such are the Hazem and the Qassaim, in the country between the Bahr-i-Nedjif and the Persian Gulf, low pebbly ridges which skirt the valley from the Bahr to below Suk-es-Sheioukh. Further west the desert becomes more stony, its surface being strewn with numerous blocks of black granite, from which it derives its appellation of Hejerra. No permanent streams water this region; occasional "wadys" or torrent-courses, only full after heavy rains, are found; but the scattered inhabitants depend for water chiefly on their wells, which are deep and numerous, but yield only a scanty supply of a brackish and unpalatable fluid. No settled population can at any time have found subsistence in this region, which produces only a few dates, and in places a poor and unsucculent herbage. Sandstorms are frequent, and at times the baleful simoon sweeps across the entire tract, destroying with its pestilential breath both men and animals.

Towards the north Chaldaea adjoined upon Assyria. From the foot of that moderately lofty range already described which the Greeks call Masius, and the modern Turks know as Jebel Tur and Karajah Dagh, extends, for above 300 miles, a plain of low elevation, slightly undulating in places, and crossed about its centre by an important limestone ridge, known as the Sinjar hills, which have a direction nearly east and west, beginning about Mosul, and terminating a little below Rakkah. This track differs from the Chaldaean lowland, by being at once less flat and more elevated. Geologically it is of secondary formation, while Chaldaea proper is tertiary or post-tertiary. It is fairly watered towards the north, but below the Sinjar is only very scantily supplied. In modern times it is for nine months in the year a desert, but anciently it was well inhabited, means having apparently been found to bring the whole into cultivation. As a complete account of this entire region must be given in another part of the present volume, this outline (it is thought) may suffice for our present purpose.

Eastward of Chaldaea, separated from it by the Tigris, which in its lower course is a stream of more body than the Euphrates, was the country known to the Jews as Elam, to the early Greeks as Cissia, and to the later Greeks as Susis or Susiana. This territory comprised a portion of the mountain country which separates Mesopotamia from Persia; but it was chiefly composed of the broad and rich flats intervening between the mountains and the Tigris, along the courses of the Kerkhah, Kuran, and Jerahi rivers. It was a rich and fertile tract, resembling Chaldaea in its general character, with the exception that the vicinity of the mountains lent it freshness, giving it cooler streams, more frequent rains, and pleasanter breezes.

Capable of maintaining with ease a dense population, it was likely, in the early times, to be a powerful rival to the Mesopotamian kingdom, over which we shall find that in fact it sometimes exercised supremacy.

On the south Chaldaea had no neighbor. Here a spacious sea, with few shoals, land-locked, and therefore protected from the violent storms of the Indian Ocean, invited to commerce, offering a ready communication with India and Ceylon, as well as with Arabia Felix, Ethiopia, and Egypt. It is perhaps to this circumstance of her geographical position, as much as to any other, that ancient Chaldaea owes her superiority over her neighbors, and her right to be regarded as one of the five great monarchies of the ancient world. Commanding at once the sea, which reaches here deep into the land, and the great rivers by means of which the commodities of the land were most conveniently brought down to the sea, she lay in the highway of trade, and could scarcely fail to profit by her position. There is sufficient reason to believe that Ur, the first capital, was a great maritime emporium; and if so, it can scarcely be doubted that to commerce and trade, at the least in part, the early development of Chaldaean greatness was owing.

CHAPTER II

CLIMATE AND PRODUCTIONS

"Ager totius Asiae fertilissimus."—PLIN. H. N. vi. 26.

Lower Mesopotamia, or Chaldaea, which lies in the same latitude with Central China, the Punjab, Palestine, Marocco, Georgia, Texas, and Central California, has a climate the warmth of which is at least equal to that of any of those regions. Even in the more northern part of the country, the district about Baghdad, the thermometer often rises during the summer to 120 deg. of Fahrenheit in the shade; and the inhabitants are forced to retreat to their serdabs or cellars, where they remain during the day, in an atmosphere which, by the entire exclusion of the sun's rays, is reduced to about 100 deg. Lower down the valley, at Zobair, Busrah, and Mohammrah, the summer temperature is still higher; and, owing to the moisture of the atmosphere, consequent on the vicinity of the sea, the heat is of that peculiarly oppressive character which prevails on the sea-coast of Hindustan, in Ceylon, in the West Indian Islands, at New Orleans, and in other places whose situation is similar. The vital powers languish under this oppression, which produces in the European a lassitude of body and a prostration of mind that wholly unfit him for active duties. On the Asiatic, however, these influences seem to have little effect. The Cha'b Arabs, who at present inhabit the region, are a tall and warlike race, strong-limbed, and muscular; they appear to enjoy the climate, and are as active, as healthy, and as long-lived as any tribe of their nation. But if man by long residence becomes thoroughly inured to the intense heat of these regions, it is otherwise with the animal creation. Camels sicken, and birds are so distressed by the high temperature that they sit in the date-trees about Baghdad, with their mouths open, panting for fresh air.

The evils proceeding from a burning temperature are augmented in places under the influence of winds, which, arising suddenly, fill the air with an impalpable sand, sometimes circling about a point, sometimes driving with furious force across a wide extent of country. The heated particles, by their contact with the atmosphere, increase its fervid glow, and, penetrating by the nose and mouth, dry up the moisture of the tongue, parch the throat, and irritate or even choke the lungs. Earth and sky are alike concealed by the dusty storm, through which no object can be distinguished that is removed many yards; a lurid gleam surrounds the traveller, and seems to accompany him as he moves: every landmark is hid from view; and to the danger of suffocation is added that of becoming bewildered and losing all knowledge of the road. Such are the perils encountered in the present condition of the country. It may be doubted, however, if in the times with which we are here concerned the evils just described had an existence. The sands of Chaldaea, which are still progressive and advancing, seem to have reached it from the Arabian Desert, to which they properly belong: year by year the drifts gain upon the alluvium, and threaten to spread over the whole country. If we may calculate the earlier by the present rate of progress, we must conclude that anciently these shifting sands had at any rate not crossed the Euphrates.

If the heat of summer be thus fierce and trying, the cold of winter must be pronounced to be very moderate. Frost, indeed, is not unknown in the country: but the frosts are only slight. Keen winds blow from the north, and in the morning the ground is often whitened by the congelation of the dew; the Arabs, impatient of a low temperature, droop and flag; but there is at no time any severity of cold; ice rarely forms in the marshes; snow is unknown; and the thermometer, even on the grass, does not often sink below 30 deg. The Persian kings passed their winter in Babylon, on account of the mildness of the climate; and Indian princes, expelled from the Peninsula, are wont, from a similar cause, to fix their residence at Busrah or Baghdad. The cold of which travellers speak is relative rather than positive. The range of the thermometer in Lower Chaldoea is perhaps 100 deg., whereas in England it is scarcely 80 deg., there is thus a greater difference between the heat of summer and the cold of winter there than here; but the actual greatest cold—that which benumbs the Arabs and makes them fall from their horses—is no more than we often experience in April, or even in May.

The rainy season of Chaldaea is in the winter time. Heavy showers fall in November, and still more in December, which sensibly raise the level of the rivers. As the spring advances the showers become lighter and less frequent; but still they recur from time to time, until the summer sets in, about May. From May to November rain is very rare indeed. The sky continues for weeks or even months without a cloud; and the sun's rays are only tempered for a short time at morning and at evening by a gray mist or haze. It is during these months that the phenomenon of the mirage is most remarkable. The strata of air, unequally heated, and therefore differing in rarity, refract the rays of light, fantastically enlarging and distorting the objects seen through them, which frequently appear raised from the ground and hanging in mid-air, or else, by a repetition of their image, which is reflected in a lower stratum, give the impression that they stand up out of a lake. Hence the delusion which has so often driven the traveller to desperation—the "image of a cool, rippling, watery mirror," which flies before him as he advances, and at once provokes and mocks his thirst.

The fertility of Chaldaea in ancient times was proverbial.

"Of all countries that we know," says Herodotus, "there is none that is so fruitful in grain. It makes no pretension, indeed, of growing the fig, the olive, the vine, or any other tree of the kind; but in grain it is so fruitful as to yield commonly two hundred-fold, and when the production is at the greatest, even three hundred-fold. The blade of the wheat-plant and of the barley-plant is often four fingers in breadth. As for the millet and the sesame, I shall not say to what height they grow, though within my own knowledge; for I am not ignorant that what I have already written concerning the fruitfulness of Babylonia must seem incredible to those who have not visited the country." Theophrastus, the disciple of Aristotle, remarks—"In Babylon the wheat-fields are regularly mown twice, and then fed off with beasts, to keep down the luxuriance of the leaf; otherwise the plant does not run to ear. When this is done, the return, in lands that are badly cultivated, is fifty-fold; while, in those that are well farmed, it is a hundred-fold." Strabo observes—"The country produces barley on a scale not known elsewhere, for the return is said to be three hundred-fold. All other wants are supplied by the palm, which furnishes not only bread, but wine, vinegar, honey, and meal." Pliny follows Theophrastus, with the exception that he makes the return of the wheat-crop, where the land is well farmed, a hundred and fifty-fold. The wealth of the region was strikingly exhibited by the heavy demands which were made upon it by the Persian kings, as well as by the riches which, notwithstanding these demands, were accumulated in the hands of those who administered its government. The money-tribute paid by Babylonia and Assyria to the Persians was a thousand talents of silver (nearly a quarter of a million of our money) annually; while the tribute in kind was reckoned at one third part of the contributions of the whole empire. Yet, despite this drain on its resources, the government was regarded as the best that the Persian king had to bestow, and the wealth accumulated by Babylonian satraps was extraordinary. Herodotus tells us of a certain Tritanteechmes, a governor, who, to his own knowledge, derived from his province nearly two bushels of silver daily! This fortunate individual had a "stud of sixteen thousand mares, with a proportionate number of horses." Another evidence of the fertility of the region may be traced in the fear of Artaxerxes Mnemon, after the battle of Cunaxa, lest the Ten Thousand should determine to settle permanently in the vicinity of Sittace upon the Tigris. Whatever opinion may be held as to the exact position of this place, and of the district intended by Xenophon, it is certain that it was in the alluvial plain and so contained within the limits of the ancient Chaldaea.

Modern travellers, speaking of Chaldaea in its present condition, express themselves less enthusiastically than the ancients; but, on the whole, agree with them as to the natural capabilities of the country. "The soil," says one of the most judicious, "is extremely fertile, producing great quantities of rice, dates, and grain of different kinds, though it is not cultivated to above half the degree of which it is susceptible." "The soil is rich," says another, "not less bountiful than that on the banks of the Egyptian Nile." "Although greatly changed by the neglect of man," observes a third, "those portions of Mesopotamia which are still cultivated, as the country about Hillah, show that the region has all the fertility ascribed to it by Herodotus." There is a general recognition of the productive qualities of the district, combined with a general lamentation over the existing neglect and apathy which allow such gifts of Nature to run to waste. Cultivation, we are told, is now the exception, instead of the rule. "Instead of the luxuriant fields, the groves and gardens of former times, nothing now meets the eye but an arid waste." Many parts of Chaldaea, naturally as productive as any others, are at present pictures of desolation. Large tracts are covered by unwholesome marshes, producing nothing but enormous reeds; others lie waste and bare, parched up by the fierce heat of the sun, and utterly destitute of water; in some places, as has been already mentioned, sand-drifts accumulate, and threaten to make the whole region a mere portion of the desert.

The great cause of this difference between ancient and modern Chaldaea is the neglect of the water-courses. Left to themselves, the rivers tend to desert some portions of the alluvium wholly, which then become utterly unproductive; while they spread themselves out over others, which are converted thereby into pestilential swamps. A well-arranged system of embankments and irrigating canals is necessary in order to develop the natural capabilities of the country, and to derive from the rich soil of this vast alluvium the valuable and varied products which it can be made to furnish.

Among the natural products of the region two stand out as pre-eminently important-the wheat-plant and the date-palm. [PLATE IV., Fig. 2.] According to the native tradition, wheat was indigenous in Chaldaea; and the first comers thus found themselves provided by the bountiful hand of Nature with the chief necessary of life. The luxuriance of the plant was excessive. Its leaves were as broad as the palm of a man's hand, and its tendency to grow leaves was so great that (as we have seen) the Babylonians used to mow it twice and then pasture their cattle on it for awhile, to keep down the blade and induce the plant to run to ear. The ultimate return was enormous; on the most moderate computation it amounted to fifty-fold at the least, and often to a hundred-fold. The modern oriental is content, even in the case of a rich soil, with a tenfold return.

The date-palm was at once one of the most valuable and one of the most ornamental products of the country. "Of all vegetable forms," says the greatest of modern naturalists, "the palm is that to which the prize of beauty has been assigned by the concurrent voice of nations in all ages." And though the date-palm is in form perhaps less graceful and lovely than some of its sister species, it possesses in the dates themselves a beauty which they lack. These charming yellow clusters, semi-transparent, which the Greeks likened to amber, and moderns compare to gold, contrast, both in shade and tint, with the green feathery branches beneath whose shade they hang, and give a richness to the landscape they adorn which adds greatly to its attractions. And the utility of the palm has been at all times proverbial. A Persian poem celebrated its three hundred and sixty uses. The Greeks, with more moderation, spoke of it as furnishing the Babylonians with bread, wine, vinegar, honey, groats, string and ropes of all kinds, firing, and a mash for fattening cattle. The fruit was excellent, and has formed at all times an important article of nourishment in the country. It was eaten both fresh and dried, forming in the latter case a delicious sweetmeat. The wine, "sweet but headachy," was probably not the spirit which it is at present customary to distil from the dates, but the slightly intoxicating drink called lagby in North Africa, which may be drawn from the tree itself by decapitating it, and suffering the juice to flow. The vinegar was perhaps the same fluid corrupted, or it may have been obtained from the dates. The honey was palm-sugar, likewise procurable from the sap. How the groats were obtained we do not know; but it appears that the pith of the palm was eaten formerly in Babylonia, and was thought to have a very agreeable flavor. Ropes were made from the fibres of the bark; and the wood was employed for building and furniture. It was soft, light and easily worked; but tough, strong and fibrous.

The cultivation of the date-palm was widely extended in Chaldaea, probably from very early times. The combination of sand, moisture, and a moderately saline soil, in which it delights, was there found in perfection, more especially in the lower country, which had but recently been reclaimed from the sea. Even now, when cultivation is almost wholly laid aside, a thick forest of luxuriant date-trees clothes the banks of the Euphrates on either side, from the vicinity of Mugheir to its embouchure at the head of the Persian Gulf. Anciently the tract was much more generally wooded with them. "Palm-trees grow in numbers over the whole of the flat country," says one of the most observant and truthful of travellers—Herodotus. According to the historians of Julian, a forest of verdure extended from the upper edge of the alluvium, which he crossed, to Mesene, and the shores of the sea. When the Arabian conquerors settled themselves in the lower country, they were so charmed with the luxuriant vegetation and the abundant date-groves, that they compared the region with the country about Damascus and reckoned it among their four earthly paradises. The propagation of the date-palm was chiefly from seed. In

Chaldaea, however, it was increased sometimes from suckers or offshoots thrown up from the stem of the old tree; at other times by a species of cutting, the entire head being struck off with about three feet of stem, notched, and then planted in moist ground. Several varieties of the tree were cultivated; but one was esteemed above all the rest, both for the size and flavor of the fruit. It bore the name of "Royal," and grew only in one place near Babylon.

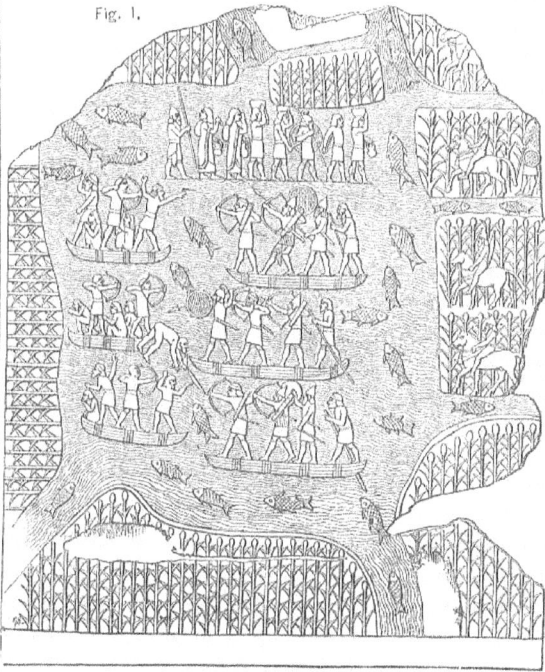

Vol I.

Plate. V.

Fig. 1.

Chaldæan Reeds (from a slab of Sennacherib).

PLATE V

Beside these two precious products, Chaldaea produced excellent barley, millet, sesame, vetches and fruits of all kinds. It was, however, deficient in variety of trees, possessing scarcely any but the palm and the cypress. Pomegranates, tamarisks, poplars, and acacias are even now almost the only trees besides the two above mentioned, to be found between Samarah and the Persian Gulf. The tamarisk grows chiefly as a shrub along the rivers, but sometimes attains the dimensions of a tree, as in the case of the "solitary tree" still growing upon the ruins of Babylon. The pomegranates with their scarlet flowers, and the acacias with their light and graceful foliage, ornament the banks of the streams, generally intermingled with the far more frequent palm, while oranges, apples, pears, and vines are successfully cultivated in the gardens and orchards.

Among the vegetable products of Chaldaea must be noticed, as almost peculiar to the region, its enormous reeds. [PLATE V.] These, which are represented with much spirit in the sculptures of Sennacherib, cover the marshes in the summer-time, rising often to the height of fourteen or fifteen feet. The Arabs of the marsh region form their houses of this material, binding the stems of the reeds together, and bending them into arches, to make the skeleton of their buildings; while, to form the walls, they stretch across from arch to arch mats made of the leaves. From the same fragile substance they construct their terradas or light boats, which, when rendered waterproof by means of bitumen, will support the weight of three or four men.

In mineral products Chaldaea was very deficient indeed. The alluvium is wholly destitute of metals, and even of stone, which must be obtained, if wanted, from the adjacent countries. The neighboring parts of Arabia could furnish sandstone and the more distant basalt; which appears to have been in fact transported occasionally to the Chaldaean Cities. Probably, however, the chief importation of stone was by the rivers, whose waters would readily convey it to almost any part of Chaldaea from the regions above the alluvium. This we know to have been done in some cases, but the evidence of the ruins makes it clear that such importation was very limited. The Chaldaeans found, in default of stone, a very tolerable material in their own country; which produced an inexhaustible supply of excellent clay, easily moulded into bricks, and not even requiring to be baked in order to fit it for the builder. Exposure to the heat of the summer sun hardened the clay sufficiently for most purposes, while a few hours in a kiln made it as firm and durable as freestone, or even granite. Chaldaea, again, yielded various substances suitable for mortar. Calcareous earths abound on the western side of the Euphrates towards the Arabian frontier; while everywhere a tenacious slime or mud is easily procurable, which, though imperfect as a cement, can serve the purpose, and has the advantage of being always at hand. Bitumen is also produced largely in some parts, particularly at Hit, where are the inexhaustible springs which have made that spot famous in all ages. Naphtha and bitumen are here given forth separately in equal abundance; and these two substances, boiled together in certain proportions, form a third kind of cement, superior to the slime or mud, but inferior to lime-mortar. Petroleum, called by the Orientals mumia, is another product of the bitumen-pits.

The wild animals indigenous in Babylonia appear to be chiefly the following:—the lion, the leopard, the hyeena, the lynx, the wild-cat, the wolf, the jackal, the wild-boar, the buffalo, the stag, the gazelle, the jerboa, the fox, the hare, the badger, and the porcupine. The Mesopotamian lion is a noble animal. Taller and larger than a Mount St. Bernard dog, he wanders over the plains their undisputed lord, unless when an European ventures to question his pre-eminence. The Arabs tremble at his approach, and willingly surrender to him the choicest of their flocks and herds. Unless urged by hunger, he seldom attacks man, but contents himself with the destruction of buffaloes, camels, dogs, and sheep. When taken young, he is easily tamed, and then manifests considerable attachment to his master. In his wild state he haunts the marshes and the banks of the various streams and canals, concealing himself during the day, and at night wandering abroad in search of his prey, to obtain which he will approach with boldness to the very skirts of an Arab encampment. His roar is not deep or terrible, but like the cry of a child in pain, or the first wail of the jackal after sunset, only louder, clearer and more prolonged. Two varieties of the lion appear to exist: the one is maneless, while the other has a long mane, which is black and shaggy. The former is now the more common in the country; but the latter, which is the fiercer of the two, is the one ordinarily represented upon the sculptures. The lioness is nearly as much feared as the lion; when her young are attacked, or when she has lost them, she is perhaps even more terrible. Her roar is said to be deeper and far more imposing than of the male.

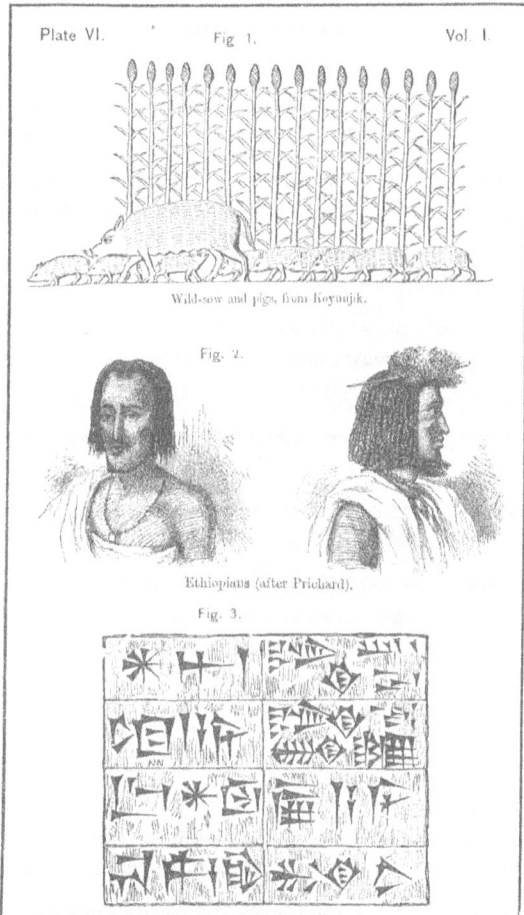

Plate VI. Fig. 1. Vol. I.

Wild-sow and pigs, from Koyunjik.

Fig. 2.

Ethiopians (after Prichard).

Fig. 3.

PLATE VI

The other animals require but few remarks. Gazelles are plentiful in the more sandy regions; buffaloes abound in the marshes of the south, where they are domesticated, and form the chief wealth of the inhabitants; troops of jackals are common, while the hyaena and wolf are comparatively rare; the wild-boar frequents the river banks and marshes, as depicted in the Assyrian sculptures [PLATE VI., Fig. 1]; hares abound in the country about Baghdad; porcupines and badgers are found in most places—leopards, lynxes, wild-cats, and deer, are somewhat uncommon.

Chaldaea possesses a great variety of birds. Falcons, vultures, kites, owls, hawks and crows of various kinds, francolins or black partridges, pelicans, wild-geese, ducks, teal, cranes, herons, kingfishers, and pigeons, are among the most common. The sand-grouse (Pterocles arenarius) is occasionally found, as also are the eagle and the bee-eater. Fish are abundant in the rivers and marshes, principally barbel and carp, which latter grow to a great size in the Euphrates. Barbel form an important element in the food of the Arabs inhabiting the Affej marshes, who take them commonly by means of a fish-spear. In the Shat-el-Arab, which is wholly within the influence of the tides, there is a species of goby, which is amphibious. This fish lies in myriads on the mud-banks left uncovered by the ebb of the tide, and moves with great agility on the approach of birds. Nature seems to have made the goby in one of her most freakish moods. It is equally at home in the earth, the air, and the water; and at different times in the day may be observed swimming in the stream, basking upon the surface of the tidal banks, and burrowing deep in the mud.

The domestic animals are camels, horses, buffaloes, cows and oxen, goats, sheep, and dogs. The most valuable of the last mentioned are grayhounds, which are employed to course the gazelle and the hare. The camels, horses, and buffaloes are of superior quality; but the cows and oxen seem to be a very inferior breed. The goats and the sheep are small, and yield a scanty supply of a somewhat coarse wool. Still their flocks and herds constitute the chief wealth of the people, who have nearly forsaken the agriculture which anciently gave Chaldaea its pre-eminence, and have relapsed very generally into a nomadic or semi-nomadic condition. The insecurity of property consequent upon bad government has in a great measure caused this change, which render; the bounty of Nature useless, and allows immense capabilities to run to waste. The present condition of Babylonia gives a most imperfect idea of its former state, which must be estimated not from modern statistics, but from the accounts of ancient writers and the evidences which he country itself presents. From them we conclude that this region was among the most productive upon the face of the earth, spontaneously producing some of the best gifts of God to man, and capable, under careful management, of being made one continuous garden.

CHAPTER III

THE PEOPLE

"A mighty nation, an ancient nation."—JEREM. v. 15.

That the great alluvial plain at the mouth of the Euphrates and Tigris was among the countries first occupied by man after the Deluge, is affirmed by Scripture, and generally allowed by writers upon ancient history. Scripture places the original occupation at a time when language had not yet broken up into its different forms, and when, consequently, races, as we now understand the term, can scarcely have existed. It is not, however, into the character of these primeval inhabitants that we have here to inquire, but into the ethnic affinities and characteristics of that race, whatever it was, which first established an important kingdom in the lower part of the plain—a kingdom which eventually became an empire. According to the ordinary theory, this race was Aramaic or Semitic. "The name of Aramaeans, Syrians, or Assyrians," says Niebuhr, "comprises the nations extending from the mouth of the Euphrates and Tigris to the Euxine, the river Halys, and Palestine. They applied to themselves the name of Aram, and the Greeks called them Assyrians, which is the same as Syrians(?). Within that great extent of country there existed, of course, various dialectic differences of language; and there can be little doubt but that in some places the nation was mixed with other races." The early inhabitants of Lower Mesopotamia, however, he considers to have been pure Aramaeans, closely akin to the Assyrians, from whom, indeed, he regards them as only separate politically.

Similar views are entertained by most modern writers. Baron Bunsen, in one of his latest works, regards the fact as completely established by the results of recent researches in Babylonia. Professor M. Muller, though expressing himself with more caution, inclines to the same conclusion. Popular works, in the shape of Cyclopaedias and short general histories, diffuse the impression. Hence a difficulty is felt with regard to the Scriptural statement concerning the first kingdom in these parts, which is expressly said to have been Cushite or Ethiopian. "And Cush begat Nimrod: (he began to be a mighty one in the earth; he was a mighty hunter before the Lord; wherefore it is said, Even as Nimrod, the mighty hunter before the Lord;) and the beginning of his kingdom was Babel, and Erech, and Accad, and Calneh, in the land of Shinar." According to this passage the early Chaldaeans should be Hamites, not Semites—Ethiopians, not Aramaans; they should present analogies and points of connection with the inhabitants of Egypt and Abyssinia, of Southern Arabia and Mekran, not with those of Upper Mesopotamia, Syria, Phoenicia, and Palestine. It will be one of the objects of this chapter to show that the Mosaical narrative conveys the exact truth—a truth alike in accordance with the earliest classical traditions, and with the latest results of modern comparative philology.

It will be desirable, however, before proceeding to establish the correctness of these assertions, to examine the grounds on which the opposite belief has been held so long and so confidently. Heeren draws his chief argument from the supposed character of the language. Assuming the form of speech called Chaldee to be the original tongue of the people, he remarks that it is "an Aramaean dialect, differing but slightly from the proper Syriac." Chaldee is known partly from the Jewish Scriptures, in which it is used occasionally, partly from the Targums (or Chaldaean paraphrases of different portions of the Sacred Volume), some of which belong to about the time of the Apostles. and partly from the two Talmuds, or collections of Jewish traditions, made in the third and fifth centuries of our era. It has been commonly regarded as the language of Babylon at the time of the Captivity, which the Jews, as captives, were forced to learn, and which thenceforth took the place of their own tongue. But it is extremely doubtful whether this is a true account of the matter. The Babylonian language of the age of Nebuchadnezzar is found to be far nearer to Hebrew than to Chaldee, which appears therefore to be misnamed, and to represent the western rather than the eastern Aramaic. The Chaldee argument thus falls to the ground: but in refuting it an admission has been made which may be thought to furnish fully as good proof of early Babylonian Semitism as the rejected theory.

It has been said that the Babylonian language in the time of Nebuchadnezzar is found to be far nearer to Hebrew than to Chaldee. It is, in fact, very close indeed to the Hebrew. The Babylonians of that period, although they did not speak the tongue known to modern linguists as Chaldee, did certainly employ a Semitic or Aramaean dialect, and so far may be set down as Semites. And this is the ground upon which such modern philologists as still maintain the Semitic character of the primitive Chaldaeans principally rely. But it can be proved from the inscriptions of the country, that between the date of the first establishment of a Chaldaean kingdom and the reign of Nebuchadnezzar, the language of Lower Mesopotamia underwent an entire change. To whatever causes this may have been owing—a subject which will be hereafter investigated—the fact is certain; and it entirely destroys the force of the argument from the language of the Babylonians at the later period.

Another ground, and that which seems to have had the chief weight with Niebuhr, is the supposed identity or intimate connection of the Babylonians with the Assyrians. That the latter people were Semites has never been denied; and, indeed, it is a point supported by such an amount of evidence as renders it quite unassailable. If, therefore the primitive Babylonians were once proved to be a mere portion of the far greater Assyrian nation, locally and politically, but not ethnically separate from them, their Semitic character would thereupon be fully established. Now that this was the belief of Herodotus must be at once allowed. Not only does that writer regard the later Babylonians as Assyrians— "Assyrians of Babylon," as he expresses it—and look on Babylonia as a mere "district of Assyria," but, by adopting the mythic genealogy, which made Ninus the son of Belus, he throws back the connection to the very origin of the two nations, and distinctly pronounces it a connection of race. But Herodotus is a very weak authority on the antiquities of any nation, even his own; and it is not surprising that he should have carried back to a remote period a state of things which he saw existing in his own age. If the later Babylonians were, in manners and customs, in religion and in language, a close, counterpart of the Assyrians, he would naturally suppose them descended from the same stock. It is his habit to transfer back to former times the condition of things in his own day. Thus he calls the inhabitants of the Peloponnese before the Dorian invasion "Dorians," regards Athens as the second city in Greece when Creesus sent his embassies, and describes as the ancient Persian religion that corrupted form which existed under Artaxerxes Longimanus. He is an excellent authority for what he had himself seen, or for what he had laboriously collected by inquiry from eye witnesses; but he had neither the critical acumen nor the linguistic knowledge necessary for the formation of a trust worthy opinion on a matter belonging to the remote history of a distant people. And the opinion of Herodotus as to the ethnic identity of the two nations is certainly not confirmed by other ancient writers. Berosus seems to have very carefully distinguished between the Assyrians and the Babylonians or Chaldaeans, as may be seen even through the doubly-distorting medium of Polyhistor and the Armenian Eusebius. Diodorus Siculus made the two nations separate and hostile in very early times. Pliny draws a clear line between the "Chaldaean races," of which Babylon was the head, and the Assyrians of the region above them. Even Herodotus in one place admits a certain amount of ethnic difference; for, in his list of the nations forming the army of Xerxes, he mentions the Chaldaeans as serving with, but not included among, the Assyrians.

The grounds, then, upon which the supposed Semitic character of the ancient Chaldaeans has been based, fail, one and all; and it remains to consider whether we have data sufficient to justify us in determinately assigning them to any other stock.

Now a large amount of tradition—classical and other—brings Ethiopians into these parts, and connects, more or less distinctly, the early dwellers upon the Persian Gulf with the inhabitants of the Nile valley, especially with those upon its upper course. Homer, speaking of the Ethiopians, says that they were "divided," and dwelt "at the ends of earth, towards the setting and the rising sun." This passage has been variously apprehended. It has been supposed to mean the mere division of the Ethiopians south of Egypt by the river Nile, whereby some inhabited its eastern and some its western bank. Again it has been explained as referring to the east and west coasts of Africa, both found by voyagers to be in the possession of Ethiopians, who were "divided" by the vast extent of continent that lay between them. But the most satisfactory explanation is that which Strabo gives from Ephorus, that the Ethiopians were considered as occupying all the south coast both of Asia and Africa, and as "divided" by the Arabian Gulf (which separated the two continents) into eastern and western-Asiatic and African. This was an "old opinion" of the Greeks, we are told; and, though Strabo thinks it indicated their ignorance, we may perhaps be excused for holding it that it might not improbably have arisen from real, though imperfect, knowledge.

The traditions with respect to Memnon serve very closely to connect Egypt and Ethiopia with the country at the head of the Persian Gulf. Memnon, King of Ethiopia, according to Hesiod and Pindar, is regarded by 'Eschylus as the son of a Cissian woman, and by Herodotus and others as the founder of Susa. He leads an army of combined Susianians and Ethiopians to the assistance of Priam, his father's brother, and, after greatly distinguishing himself, perishes in one of the battles before Troy. At the same time he is claimed as one of their monarchs by the Ethiopians upon the Nile, and identified by the Egyptians with their king, Amunoph III., whose statue became known as "the vocal Memnon." Sometimes his expedition is supposed to have started from the African Ethiopia, and to have proceeded by way of Egypt to its destination. There were palaces, called "Memnonia," and supposed to have been built by him, both in Egypt and at Susa; and there was a tribe, called Memnones, near Meroe. Memnon thus unites the Eastern and the Western Ethiopians; and the less we regard him as an historical personage, the more must we view him as personifying the ethnic identity of the two races.

The ordinary genealogies containing the name of Belus point in the same direction, and serve more definitely to connect the Babylonians with the Cushites of the Nile. Pherecydes, who is an earlier writer than Herodotus, makes Agenor, the son of Neptune, marry Damno, the daughter of Belus, and have issue Phoenix, Isaea, and Melia, of whom Melia marries Danaus, and Isaea Aegyptus. Apollodorus, the disciple of Eratosthenes, expresses the connection thus:—"Neptune took to wife Libya (or Africa), and had issue Belus and Agenor. Belus married Anchinoe, daughter of Nile, who gave birth to AEgyptus, Danaus, Cepheus, and Phineus. Agenor married Telephassa, and had issue Europa, Cadmus, Phoenix, and Cilix." Eupolemus, who professes to record the Babylonian tradition on the subject, tells us that the first Belus, whom he identifies with Saturn, had two sons, Belus and Canaan. Canaan begat the progenitor of the Phoenicians (Phoenix?), who had two sons, Chum and Mestraim, the ancestors respectively of the Ethiopians and the Egyptians. Charax of Pergamus spoke of AEgyptus as the son of Belus. John of Antioch agrees with Apollodorus, but makes certain additions. According to him, Neptune and Lybia had three children, Agenor, Belus, and Enyalius or Mars. Belus married Sida, and had issue AEgyptus and Danaus; while Agenor married Tyro, and became the father of five children—Cadmus, Phoenix, Syrus, Cilix, and Europa.

Many further proofs might be adduced, were they needed, of the Greek belief in an Asiatic Ethiopia, situated somewhere between Arabia and India, on the shores of the Erythraean Sea. Herodotus twice speaks of the Ethiopians of Asia, whom he very carefully distinguishes from those of Africa, and who can only be sought in this position. Ephorus, as we have already seen, extended the Ethiopians along the whole of the coast washed by the Southern Ocean. Eusebius has preserved a tradition that, in the reign of Amenophis III., a body of Ethiopians migrated from the country about the Indus, and settled in the valley of the Nile. Hesiod and Apollodorus, by making Memnon, the Ethiopian king, son of the Dawn (Greek) imply their belief in an Ethiopia situated to the east rather than to the south of Greece. These are a few out of the many similar notices which it would be easy to produce from classical writers, establishing, if not the fact itself, yet at any rate a full belief in the fact on the part of the best informed among the ancient Greeks.

The traditions of the Armenians are in accordance with those of the Greeks. The Armenian Geography applies the name of Cush, or Ethiopia, to the four great regions, Media, Persia, Susiana or Elymais, and Aria, or to the whole territory between the Indus and the Tigris. Moses of Chorene, the great Armenian historian, identifies Belus, King of Babylon, with Nimrod; while at the same time he adopts for him a genealogy only slightly different from that in our present copies of Genesis, making Nimrod the grandson of Cush, and the son of Mizraim. He thus connects, in the closest way, Babylonia, Egypt, and Ethiopia Proper, uniting moreover, by his identification of Nimrod with Belus, the Babylonians of later times who worshipped Belus as their hero-founder, with the primitive population introduced into the country by Nimrod.

The names of Belus and Cush, thus brought into juxtaposition, have remained attached to some portion or other of the region in question from ancient times to the present day. The tract immediately east of the Tigris was known to the Greeks as Cissia or Cossaea, no less than as Elymais or Elam. The country east of Kerman was named Kusan throughout the Sassanian period. The same region is now Beloochistan, the country of the Belooches or Belus, while adjoining it on the east is Cutch, or Kooch, a term standing to Cush is Belooch stands to Belus. Again, Cissia or Cossaea is now Khuzistan, or the land of Khuz a name not very remote from Cush; but perhaps this is only a coincidence.

To the traditions and traces here enumerated must be added, as of primary importance, the Biblical tradition, which is delivered to us very simply and plainly in that precious document the "Toldoth Beni Noah," or "Book of the Generations of the Sons of Noah," which well deserves to be called "the most authentic record that we possess for the affiliation of nations." "The sons of Ham," we are told, "were Cush, and Mizraim, and Phut, and Canaan . . . . And Cush begat Nimrod . . . . And the beginning of his kingdom was Babel, and Erech, and Accad, and Calneh, in the land of Shinar." Here a primitive Babylonian kingdom is assigned to a people distinctly said to have been Cushite by blood, and to have stood in close connection with Mizraim, or the people of Egypt, Phut, or those of Central Africa, and Canaan, or those of Palestine. It is the simplest and the best interpretation of this passage to understand it as asserting that the four races—the Egyptians, Ethiopians, Libyans, and Canaanites—were ethnically connected, being all descended from Ham; and further, that the primitive people of Babylon were a subdivision of one of these races, namely of the Cushites or Ethiopians, connected in some degree with the Canaanites, Egyptians, and Libyans, but still more closely with the people which dwelt anciently upon the Upper Nile.

The conclusions thus recommended to us by the consentient primitive traditions of so many races, have lately received most important and unexpected confirmation from the results of linguistic research. After the most remarkable of the Mesopotamian mounds had yielded their treasures, and supplied the historical student with numerous and copious documents bearing upon the history of the great Assyrian and Babylonian empires, it was determined to explore Chaldaea Proper, where mounds of less pretension, but still of considerable height, marked the sites of a number of ancient cities. The excavations conducted at these places, especially at Niffer, Senkereh, Warka, and Mugheir, were eminently successful. Among their other unexpected results was the discovery, in the most ancient remains, of a new form of speech, differing greatly from the later Babylonian language and presenting analogies with the early language of Susiana, as well as with that of the second column of the Achoemenian inscriptions. In grammatical structure this ancient tongue resembles dialects of the Turanian family, but its vocabulary has been pronounced to be "decidedly Cushite or Ethiopian;" and the modern languages to which it approaches the nearest are thought to be the Mahra of Southern Arabia and the Galla of Abyssinia. Thus comparative philology appears to confirm the old traditions. An Eastern Ethiopia instead of being the invention of bewildered ignorance, is rather a reality which henceforth it will require a good deal of scepticism to doubt; and the primitive race which bore sway in Chaldaea Proper is with much probability assigned to this ethnic type. The most striking physical characteristics of the African Ethiopians were their swart complexions, and their crisp or frizzled hair. According to Herodotus the Asiatic Ethiopian: were equally dark, but their hair was straight and not frizzled. Probably in neither case was the complexion what we understand by black, but rather a dark red-brown or copper color, which is the tint of the modern Gallas and Abyssinians, as well as of the Cha'b and Montefik Arabs and the Belooches. The hair was no doubt abundant; but it was certainly not woolly like that of the negroes. There is a marked distinction between the negro hair and that of the Ethiopian race, which is sometimes straight, sometimes crisp, but never woolly. This distinction is carefully marked in the Egyptian monuments, as is also the distinction between the Ethiopian and negro complexions; whence we may conclude that there was as much difference between the two races in ancient as in modern times. The African races descended from the Ethiopians are on the whole a handsome rather than an ugly people; their figure is slender and well shaped; their features are regular, and have some delicacy; the forehead is straight and fairly high; the nose long, straight, and fine, but scarcely so prominent as that of Europeans; the chin is pointed and good. [PLATE VI., Fig. 2.]

The principal defect is in the mouth, which has lips too thick and full for beauty, though they are not turned out like a negro's. We do not possess any representations of the ancient people which can be distinctly assigned to the early Cushite period. Abundant hair has been noticed in an early tomb; and this in the later Babylonians, who must have been descended in great part from the earlier, was very conspicuous; but otherwise we have as yet no direct evidence with respect to the physical characteristics of the primitive race. That they were brave and warlike, ingenious, energetic, and persevering, we have ample evidence, which will appear in later chapters of this work; but we can do little more than conjecture their physical appearance, which, however, we may fairly suppose to have resembled that of other Ethiopian nations.

When the early inhabitants of ChaldAea are pronounced to have belonged to the same race with the dwellers upon the Upper Nile, the question naturally arises, which were the primitive people, and which the colonists? Is the country at the head of the Persian Gulf to be regarded as the original abode of the Cushite race, whence it spread eastward and westward, on the one hand to Susiana, Persia Proper, Carmania, Gedrosia, and India itself; on the other to Arabia and the east coast of Africa? Or are we to suppose that the migration proceeded in one direction only—that the Cushites, having occupied the country immediately to the south of Egypt, sent their colonies along the south coast of Arabia, whence they crept on into the Persian Gulf, occupying Chaldaea and Susiana, and thence spreading into Mekran, Kerman, and the regions bordering upon the Indus? Plausible reasons maybe adduced in support of either hypothesis. The situation of Babylonia, and its proximity to that mountain region where man must have first "increased and multiplied" after the Flood, are in favor of its being the original centre from which the other Cushite races were derived. The Biblical genealogy of the sons of Ham points, however, the other way; for it derives Nimrod from Cush, not Cush from Nimrod. Indeed this document seems to follow the Hamites from Africa—emphatically "the land of Ham"—in one line along Southern Arabia to Shinar or Babylonia, in another from Egypt through Canaan into Syria. The antiquity of civilization in the valley of the Nile, which preceded by many centuries that even of primitive Chaldaea, is another argument in favor of the migration having been from west to east; and the monuments and traditions of the Chaldaeans themselves have been thought to present some curious indications of an East African origin. On the whole, therefore, it seems most probable that the race designated in Scripture by the hero-founder Nimrod, and among the Greeks by the eponym of Belus, passed from East Africa, by way of Arabia, to the valley of the Euphrates, shortly before the opening of the historical period.

Upon the ethnic basis here indicated, there was grafted, it would seem, at a very early period, a second, probably Turanian, element, which very importantly affected the character and composition of the people. The Burbur or Akkad, who are found to have been a principal tribe under the early kings, are connected by name, religion, and in some degree by language, with an important people of Armenia, called Burbur and Urarda, the Alarodians (apparently) of Herodotus. It has been conjectured that this race at a very remote date descended upon the plain country, conquering the original Cushite inhabitants, and by degrees blending with them, though the fusion remained incomplete to the time of Abraham. The language of the early inscriptions, though Cushite in its vocabulary, is Turanian in many points of its grammatical structure, as in its use of post-positions, particles, and pronominal suffixes; and it would seem, therefore, scarcely to admit of a doubt that the Cushites of Lower Babylon must in some way or other have become mixed with a Turanian people. The mode and time of the commixture are matters altogether beyond our knowledge. We can only note the fact as indicated by the phenomena, and form, or abstain from forming, as we please, hypotheses with respect to its accompanying circumstances.

Besides these two main constituents of the Chaldaean race, there is reason to believe that both a Semitic and an Arian element existed in the early population of the country. The subjects of the early kings are continually designated in the inscriptions by the title of kiprat-arbat, "the four nations," or arba lisun, "the four tongues." In Abraham's time, again, the league of four kings seems correspondent to a fourfold ethnic division, Cushite, Turanian, Semitic, and Arian, the chief authority and ethnic preponderance being with the Cushites. The language also of the early inscriptions is thought to contain traces of Semitic and Arian influence; so that it is at least probable that the "four tongues" intended were not mere local dialects, but distinct languages, the representatives respectively of the four great families of human speech.

It would result from this review of the linguistic facts and other ethnic indications, that the Chaldaeans were not a pure, but a very mixed people. Like the Romans in ancient and the English in modern Europe, they were a "colluvio gentium omnium," a union of various races between which there was marked and violent contrast. It is now generally admitted that such races are among those which play the most distinguished part in the world's history, and most vitally affect its progress.

With respect to the name of Chaldaean, under which it has been customary to designate this mixed people, it is curious to find that in the native documents of the early period it does not occur at all. Indeed it first appears in the Assyrian inscriptions of the ninth century before our era, being then used as the name of the dominant race in the country about Babylon. Still, as Berosus, who cannot easily have been ignorant of the ancient appellation of his race, applies the term Chaldaean to the primitive people, and as Scripture assigns Ur to the Chaldees as early as the time of Abraham, we are entitled to assume that this term, whenever it came historically into use, is in fact no unfit designation for the early inhabitants of the country. Perhaps the most probable account of the origin of the word is that it designates properly the inhabitants of the ancient capital, Ur or Hur-Khaldi being in the Burbur dialect the exact equivalent of Hur, which was the proper name of the Moon-God, and Chaldaeans being thus either "Moon-worshippers," or simply "inhabitants of the town dedicated to, and called after, the Moon." Like the term "Babylonian," it would at first have designated simply the dwellers in the capital, and would subsequently have been extended to the people generally.

A different theory has of late years been usually maintained with respect to the Chaldaeans. It has been supposed that they were a race entirely distinct from the early Babylonians—Armenians, Arabs, Kurds, or Sclaves —who came down from the north long after the historical period, and settled as the dominant race in the lower Mesopotamian valley. Philological arguments of the weakest and most unsatisfactory character were confidently adduced in support of these views; but they obtained acceptance chiefly on account of certain passages of Scripture, which were thought to imply that the Chaldaeans first colonized Babylonia in the seventh or eighth century before Christ. The most important of these passages is in Isaiah. That prophet, in his denunciation of woe upon Tyre, says, according to our translation,—"Behold the land of the Chaldaeans this people was not, till the Assyrian founded it for them that dwell in the wilderness; they set up the towers thereof, they raised up the palaces thereof; and he brought it to ruin;" or, according to Bishop Lowth, "Behold the land of the Chaldaeans. This people was of no account. (The Assyrians founded it for the inhabitants of the desert, they raised the watch-towers, they setup the palaces thereof.) This people hath reduced her and shall reduce her to ruin." It was argued that we had here a plain declaration that, till a little before Isaiah's time, the Chaldaeans had never existed as a nation. Then, it was said, they obtained for the first time fixed habitations from one of the Assyrian kings, who settled them in a city, probably Babylon. Shortly afterwards, following the analogy of so many Eastern races, they suddenly sprang up to power. Here another passage of Scripture was thought to have an important bearing on their history. "Lo! I raise up the Chaldaeans," says Habakkuk, "that bitter and hasty nation, which shall march through the breadth of the land to possess the dwelling places that are not theirs. They are terrible and dreadful; their judgment and their dignity shall proceed of themselves; their horses also are swifter than the leopards, and are more fierce than the evening wolves: and their horsemen shall spread themselves, and their horsemen shall come from far; they shall fly as an eagle that hasteth to eat; they shall come all for violence; their faces shall nip as the east wind, and they shall gather the captivity as the sand. And they shall scoff at the kings, and the princes shall be a scorn unto them; they shall deride every stronghold; they shall heap dust and take it." The Chaldaeans, recent occupants of Lower Mesopotamia, and there only a dominant race, like the Normans in England or the Lombards in North Italy, were, on a sudden, "raised" elevated from their low estate of Assyrian colonists to the conquering people which they became under Nebuchadnezzar.

Such was the theory, originally advanced by Gesenius, which, variously modified by other writers, held its ground on the whole as the established view, until the recent cuneiform discoveries. It was, from the first, a theory full of difficulty. The mention of the Chaldaeans in Job, and even in Genesis, as a well-known people, was in contradiction to the supposed recent origin of the race. The explanation of the obscure passage in the 23d chapter of Isaiah, on which the theory was mainly based, was at variance with other clearer passages of the same prophet. Babylon is called by Isaiah the "daughter of the Chaldaeans," and is spoken of as an ancient city, long "the glory of kingdoms," the oppressor of nations, the power that "smote the people in wrath with a continual stroke." She is "the lady of kingdoms," and "the beauty of the Chaldees' excellency." The Chaldaeans are thus in Isaiah, as elsewhere generally in Scripture, the people of Babylonia, the term "Babylonians" not being used by him; Babylon is their chief city, not one which they have conquered and occupied, but their "daughter"—"the beauty of their excellency;" and so all the antiquity and glory which is assigned to Babylon belong necessarily in Isaiah's mind to the Chaldaeans. The verse, therefore, in the 23d chapter, on which so much has been built, can at most refer to some temporary depression of the Chaldaeans, which made it a greater disgrace to Tyre that she should be conquered by them. Again, the theory of Gesenius took no account of the native historian, who is (next to Scripture) the best literary authority for the facts of Babylonian history. Berosus not only said nothing of any influx of an alien race into Babylonia shortly before the time of Nebuchadnezzar, but pointedly identified the Chaldaeans of that period with the primitive people of the country. Nor can it be said that he would do this from national vanity, to avoid the confession of a conquest, for he admits no fewer than three conquests of Babylon, a "Midian, an Arabian, and an

Assyrian." Thus, even apart from the monuments, the theory in question would be untenable. It really originated in linguistic speculations, which turn out to have been altogether mistaken.

The joint authority of Scripture and of Berosus will probably be accepted as sufficient to justify the adoption of a term which, if not strictly correct, is yet familiar to us, and which will conveniently serve to distinguish the primitive monarchy, whose chief seats were in Chaldaea Proper (or the tract immediately bordering upon the Persian Gulf), from the later Babylonian Empire, which had its head-quarters further to the north. The people of this first kingdom will therefore be called Chaldaeans, although there is no evidence that they applied the name to themselves, or that it was even known to them in primitive times.

The general character of this remarkable people will best appear from the account, presently to be given, of their manners, their mode of life, their arts, their science, their religion, and their history. It is not convenient to forestall in this place the results of almost all our coming inquiries. Suffice it to observe that, though possessed of not many natural advantages, the Chaldaean people exhibited a fertility of invention, a genius, and an energy which place them high in the scale of nations, and more especially in the list of those descended from a Hamitic stock. For the last 3000 years the world has been mainly indebted for its advancement to the Semitic and Indo-European races; but it was otherwise in the first ages. Egypt and Babylon—Mizraim and Nimrod—both descendants of Ham—led the way, and acted as the pioneers of mankind in the various untrodden fields of art, literature, and science. Alphabetic writing, astronomy, history, chronology, architecture, plastic art, sculpture, navigation, agriculture, textile industry, seem, all of them, to have had their origin in one or other of these two countries. The beginnings may have been often humble enough. We may laugh at the rude picture-writing, the uncouth brick pyramid, the coarse fabric, the homely and ill-shapen instruments, as they present themselves to our notice in the remains of these ancient nations; but they are really worthier of our admiration than of our ridicule. The first inventors of any art are among the greatest benefactors of their race; and the bold step which they take from the unknown to the known, from blank ignorance to discovery, is equal to many steps of subsequent progress. "The commencement," says Aristotle, "is more than half of the whole." This is a sound judgment; and it will be well that we should bear it in mind during the review, on which we are about to enter, of the language, writing, useful and ornamental art, science, and literature of the Chaldaeans. "The child is father of the man," both in the individual and the species; and the human race at the present day lies under infinite obligations to the genius and industry of early ages.

CHAPTER IV

LANGUAGE AND WRITING

It was noted in the preceding chapter that Chaldaea, in the earliest times to which we can go back, seems to have been inhabited by four principal tribes. The early kings are continually represented on the monuments as sovereigns over the Kiprat-arbat, or, Four Races. These "Four Races" are called sometimes the Arba Lisun, or "Four Tongues," whence we may conclude that they were distinguished from one another, among other differences, by a variety in their forms of speech. The extent and nature of the variety could not, of course, be determined merely from this expression; but the opinion of those who have most closely studied the subject appears to be that the differences were great and marked-the languages in fact belonging to the four great varieties of human speech—Hamitic, Semitic, Arian, and Turanian.

The language which the early inscriptions have revealed to us is not, of course, composed equally of these four elements. It does, however, contain strong marks of admixture. It is predominantly Cushite in its vocabulary, Turanian in its structure. Its closest analogies are with such dialects as the Mahra of Arabia, the Galla and Wolaitsa of Abyssinia, and the ancient language of Egypt, but in certain cases it more resembles the Turkish. Tatar, and Magyar (Turanian) dialects; while in some it presents Semitic and in others Arian affinities. This will appear sufficiently from the following list:

Dingir, or Dimir, "God." Compare Turkish Tengri.
Atta, "father." Compare Turkish atta. Etea is "father" in the Wolaitsa (Abyssinian) dialect.
Sis, "brother." Compare Wolaitsa and Woratta isha.
Tur, "a youth," "a son," Compare the tur-khan of the Parthians (Turanians), who was the Crown Prince.
E, "a house." Compare ancient Egyptian e, and Turkish ev.
Ka, "a gate." Compare Turkish kapi.
Kharran, "a road." Compare Galla kara.
Huru, "a town." Compare Heb. [—]
Ar, "a river." Compare Heb. [—], Arab. nahr.
Gabri, "a mountain." Compare Arabic jabal.
Ki, "the earth."
Kingi, "a country."
San, "the sun."
Kha, "a fish"(?).
Kurra, "a horse." Compare Arabic gurra.
Guski, "gold." Compare Galla irerke. Guski means also "red" and "the evening."
Babar, "silver," "white," "the morning." Compare Agau ber, Tigre burrur.
Zabar, "copper." Compare Arabic sifr.
Hurud, "iron." Compare Arabic hadid.
Zakad, "the head." Compare Gonga toko.
Kat, "the hand." Compare Gonga kiso.
Si, "the eye."
Pi, "the ear." Compare Magyar ful.
Gula, "great." Compare Galla guda.
Tura, "little." Compare Gonga tu and Galla tina.
Kelga, "powerful."
Ginn, "first."
Mis, "many." Compare Agau minch or mench.
Gar, "to do."
Egir, "after." Compare Hhamara (Abyssinian) igria.

The grammar of this language is still but very little known. The conjugations of verbs are said to be very intricate and difficult, a great variety of verbal forms being from the same root as in Hebrew, by means of preformatives. Number and person in the verbs are marked by suffixes—the third person singular (masculine) by bi (compare Gonga bi, "he"), or ani (compare Galla enni, "he"), the third person plural by bi-nini.

The accusative case in nouns is marked by a postposition, ku, as in Hindustani. The plural of pronouns and substantives is formed sometimes by reduplication. Thus ni is "him," while nini is "them;" and Chanaan, Yavnan, Libnan seem to be plural forms from Chna, Yavan and Liban.

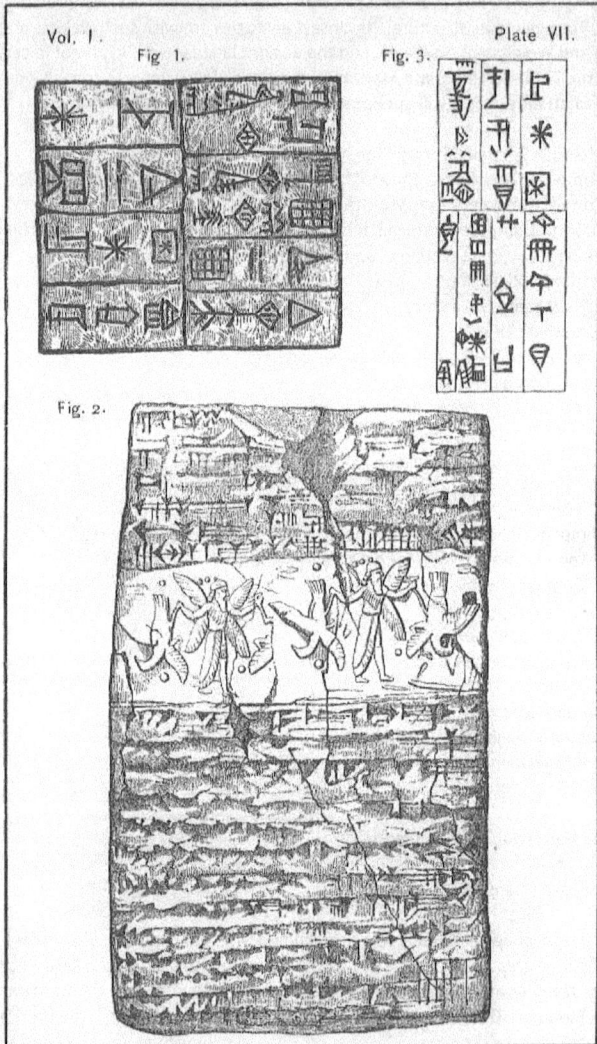

PLATE VII

A curious anomaly occurs in the declension of pronouns.' When accompanied by the preposition kita, "with," there is a tmesis of the preposition, and the pronouns are placed between its first and second syllable; e.g. vi, him''-ki-ni-ta, "with him." This takes place in every number and person, as the following scheme will show:—

	1st person.	2d person.	3d person.
Sing.	ki-mu-ta (with me)	ki-zu-ta (with thee)	ki-ni-ta (with him)
Plur.	ki mi-ta (with us)	ki zu-nini-ta (with you)	ki-nini-ta (with them)

N. B.—The formation of the second person plural deserves attention. The word zu-nini is, clearly, composed of the two elements, zu, "thee," and nini, "them"—so that instead of having a word for "you," the Chaldaeans employed for it the periphrasis "thee-them"! There is, I believe, no known language which presents a parallel anomaly.

Such are the chief known features of this interesting but difficult form of speech. A specimen may now be given of the mode in which it was written. Among the earliest of the monuments hitherto discovered are a set of bricks bearing the following cuneiform inscription [PLATE VI., Fig. 3]:

This inscription is explained to mean:—"Beltis, his lady, has caused Urukh (?), the pious chief, King of Hur, and King of the land (?) of the Akkad, to build a temple to her." In the same locality where it occurs, bricks are also found bearing evidently the same inscription, but written in a different manner. Instead of the wedge and arrow-head being the elements of the writing, the whole is formed by straight lines of almost uniform thickness, and the impression seems to have been made by a single stamp. [PLATE VII., Fig. 1.]

This mode of writing, which has been called without much reason "the hieratic," and of which we have but a small number of instances, has confirmed a conjecture, originally suggested by the early cuneiform writing itself, that the characters were at first the pictures of objects. In some cases the pictorial representation is very plain and palpable.

For instance, the "determinative" of a god—the sign that is, which marks that the name of a god is about to follow, in this early rectilinear writing is ✳, an eight-rayed star. The archaic cuneiform keeps closely to this type, merely changing the lines into wedges, thus ✳, while the later cuneiform first unites the oblique wedges in one ✳, and then omits them as unnecessary, retaining only the perpendicular and the horizontal ones ⊤.

Again, the character representing the word "hand" is, in the rectilinear writing ⊟, in the archaic cuneiform ⊟, in the later cuneiform ⊟. The five lines (afterwards reduced to four) clearly represent the thumb and the four fingers. So the character ordinarily representing "a house" ▱ is evidently formed from the original ▭, the ground-plan of a house; and that denoting "the sun" ◄, comes from ◇, through ◈, and ◈, the original ◇ being the best representation that straight lines could give of the sun. In the case of *ka*, "a gate," we have not the original design; but we may see posts, bars, and hinges in ▤, the ordinary character.[4]

Another curious example of the pictorial origin of the letters is furnished by the character [—] , which is the French une, the feminine of "one." This character may be traced up through several known forms to an original picture, which is thus given on a Koyunjik tablet [—] . It has been conjectured that the object here represented is "a sarcophagus." But the true account seems to be that it is a double-toothed comb, a toilet article peculiar to women, and therefore one which might well be taken to express "a woman," or more generally the feminine gender. It is worth notice that the emblem is the very one still in use among the Lurs, in the mountains overhanging Babylonia. And it is further remarkable that the phonetic power of the character here spoken of is it (or yat) the ordinary Semitic feminine ending.

The original writing, it would therefore seem, was a picture-writing as rude as that of the Mexicans. Objects were themselves represented, but coarsely and grotesquely—and, which is especially remarkable, without any curved lines. This would seem to indicate that the system grew up where a hard material, probably stone, was alone used. The cuneiform writing arose when clay took the place of stone as a material. A small tool with a square or triangular point, impressed, by a series of distinct touches, the outline of the old pictured objects on the soft clay of tablets and bricks. In course of time simplifications took place. The less important wedges were omitted. One stroke took the place of two, or sometimes of three. In this way the old form of objects became, in all but a few cases, very indistinct; while generally it was lost altogether.

Originally each character had, it would seem, the phonetic power of the name borne by the object which it represented. But, as this namee was different in the languages of the different tribes inhabiting the country, the same character came often to have several distinct phonetic values. For instance, the character [—] representing "a house," had the phonetic values of e, bit, and mal, because those were the words expressive of "a house," among the Hamitic, Semitic, and Arian populations respectively. Again, characters did not always retain their original phonetic powers, but abbreviated them. Thus the character which originally stood for Assur, "Assyria," came to have the sound of as, that denoting bil, "a lord," had in addition the sound of bi, and so on. Under these circumstances it is almost impossible to feel any certainty in regard to the phonetic representation of a single line of these old inscriptions. The meaning of each word may be well known; but the articulate sounds which were in the old times attached to them may be matter almost of conjecture.

The Chaldaean characters are of three kinds-letters proper, monograms, and determinatives. With regard to the letters proper, there is nothing particular to remark, except that they have almost always a syllabic force. The monograms represent in a brief way, by a wedge or a group of wedges, an entire word, often of two or three syllables, as Nebo, Babil, Merodach, etc. The determinatives mark that the word which they accompany is a word of a certain class, as a god, a man, a country, a town, etc. These last, it is probable, were not sounded at all when the word was read. They served, in some degree, the purpose of our capital letters, in the middle of sentences, but gave more exact notice of the nature of the coming word. Curiously enough, they are retained sometimes, where the word which they accompany has merely its phonetic power, as (generally) when the names of gods form a part of the names of monarchs.

It has been noticed already that the chief material on which the ancient Chaldaeans wrote was moist clay, in the two forms of tablets and bricks. On bricks are found only royal inscriptions, having reference to the building in which the bricks were used, commonly designating its purpose, and giving the name and titles of the-monarch who erected it. The inscription does not occupy the whole brick, but a square or rectangular space towards its centre. It is in some cases stamped, in some impressed with a tool. The writing—as in all cuneiform inscriptions, excepting those upon seals—is from left to right, and the lines are carefully separated from one another. Some specimens have been already given.

The tablets of the Chaldaeans are among the most remarkable of their remains, and will probably one day throw great additional light on the manners and customs, the religion, and even, perhaps, the science and learning, of the people. They are small pieces of clay, somewhat rudely shaped into a form resembling a pillow, and thickly inscribed with cuneiform characters, which are sometimes accompanied by impressions of the cylindrical seals so common in the museums of Europe. The seals are rolled across the body of the document, as in the accompanying figure. [PLATE VII., Fig. 2.] Except where these impressions occur, the clay is commonly covered on both sides with minute writing. What is most curious, however, is that the documents thus duly attested have in general been enveloped, after they were baked, in a cover of moist clay, upon which their contents have been again inscribed, so as to present externally a duplicate of the writing within; and the tablet in its cover has then been baked afresh. That this was the process employed is evident from the fact that the inner side of the envelope bears a cast, in relief, of the inscription beneath it. Probably the object in view was greater security— that if the external cover became illegible, or was tampered with, there might be a means of proving beyond a doubt what the document actually contained. The tablets in question have in a considerable number of cases been deciphered; they are for the most part deeds, contracts, or engagements, entered into by private persons and preserved among the archives of families.

Besides their writings on clay, the Chaldaeans were in the habit, from very early times, of engraving inscriptions on gems. The signet cylinder of a very ancient king exhibits that archaic formation of letters which has been already noted as appearing upon some of the earliest bricks. [PLATE VII., Fig. 3.] That it belongs to the same period is evident, not only from the resemblance of the literal type, but from the fact that the same king's name appears upon both. This signet inscription—so far as it has been hitherto deciphered—is read as follows:—"The signet of Urukh, the pious chief, king of Ur, ... High-Priest (?) of . . . . Niffer." Another similar relic, belonging to a son of this monarch, has the inscription, "To the manifestation of Nergal, king of Bit-Zida, of Zurgulla, for the saving of the life of Ilgi, the powerful hero, the king of Ur, ... son of Urukh . . . . May his name be preserved." A third signet, which belongs to a later king in the series, bears the following legend: "—sin, the powerful chief, the king of Ur, the king of the Kiprat-arbat (or four races) . . . . his seal." The cylinders, however, of this period are more usually without inscriptions, being often plain, and often engraved with figures, but without a legend.

CHAPTER V

ARTS AND SCIENCES

"Chaldaei cognitione astrorum sollertiaque ingeniorum antecellunt." Cic. de Div. i. 41.

Among the arts which the first Ethiopic settlers on the shores of the Persian Gulf either brought with them from their former homes, or very early invented in their new abode, must undoubtedly have been the two whereby they were especially characterized in the time of their greatest power—architecture and agriculture. Chaldaea is not a country disposing men to nomadic habits. The productive powers of the soil would at once obtrude themselves on the notice of the new comers, and would tempt to cultivation and permanency of residence. If the immigrants came by sea, and settled first in the tract immediately bordering upon the gulf, as seems to have been the notion of Berosus, their earliest abodes may have been of that simple character which can even now be witnessed in the Affej and Montefik marshes—that is to say, reed cabins, supported by the tall stems of the growing plants bent into arches, and walled with mats composed of flags or sedge. Houses of this description last for forty or fifty years and would satisfy the ideas of a primitive race. When greater permanency began to be required, palm-beams might take the place of the reed supports, and wattles plastered with mud that of the rush mats; in this way habitations would soon be produced quite equal to those in which the bulk of mankind reside, even at the present day.

In process of time however, a fresh want would be felt. Architecture, as has been well observed, has its origin, not in nature only, but in religion. The common worship of God requires temples; and it is soon desired to give to these sacred edifices a grandeur, a dignity, and a permanency corresponding to the nature of the Being worshipped in them. Hence in most countries recourse is had to stone, as the material of greatest strength and durability; and by its means buildings are raised which seem almost to reach the heaven whereof they witness. In Babylonia, as it has been already observed, this material was entirely wanting. Nowhere within the limits of the alluvium was a quarry to be found; and though at no very great distance, on the Arabian border, a coarse sandstone might have been obtained, yet in primitive times, before many canals were made, the difficulty of transporting this weighty substance across the soft and oozy soil of the plain would necessarily have prevented its adoption generally, or, indeed, anywhere, except in the immediate vicinity of the rocky region. Accordingly we find that stone was never adopted in Babylonia as a building material, except to an extremely small extent; and that the natives were forced, in its default, to seek for the grand edifices, which they desired to build, a different substance.

The earliest traditions, and the existing remains of the earliest buildings, alike inform us that the material adopted was brick. An excellent clay is readily procurable in all parts of the alluvium; and this, when merely exposed to the intense heat of an Eastern sun for a sufficient period, or still more when kiln-dried, constitutes a very tolerable substitute for the stone employed by most nations. The baked bricks, even of the earliest tines, are still sound and hard; while the sun-dried bricks, though they have often crumbled to dust or blended together in one solid earthen mass, yet sometimes retain their shape and original character almost unchanged, and offer a stubborn resistance to the excavator. In the most ancient of the Chaldaean edifices we occasionally find, as in the Bowariyeh ruin at Warka, the entire structure composed of the inferior material; but the more ordinary practice is to construct the mass of the building in this way, and then to cover it completely with a facing of burnt brick, which sometimes extends to as much as ten feet in thickness. The burnt brick was thus made to protect the unburnt from the influence of the weather, while labor and fuel—were greatly economized by the employment to so large an extent of the natural substance. The size and color of the bricks vary. The general shape is square, or nearly so, while the thickness is, to modern ideas, disproportionately small; it is not, however, so small as in the bricks of the Romans. The earliest of the baked bricks hitherto discovered in Chaldaea are 11 1/4 inches square, and 2 1/2 inches thick, while the Roman are often 15 inches square, and only an inch and a quarter thick. The baked bricks of later date are of larger size than the earlier; they are commonly about 13 inches square, with a thickness of three inches. The best quality of baked brick is of a yellowish-white tint, and very much resembles our Stourbridge or fire brick; another kind, extremely hard, but brittle, is of a blackish blue; a third, the coarsest of all, is slack-dried, and of a pale red. The earliest baked bricks are of this last color. The sun-dried bricks have even more variety of size than the baked ones. They are sometimes as large as 16 inches square and seven inches thick, sometimes as small as six inches square by two thick. Occasionally, though not very often, bricks are found differing altogether in shape from those above described, being formed for special purposes. Of this kind are the triangular bricks used at the corners of walls, intended to give greater regularity to the angles than would otherwise be attained; and the wedge-shaped bricks, formed to be employed in arches, which were known and used by this primitive people.

The modes of applying these materials to building purposes were various. Sometimes the crude and the burnt brick were used in alternate layers, each layer being several feet in thickness; more commonly the crude brick was used (as already noticed) for the internal parts of the building, and a facing of burnt brick protected the whole from the weather. Occasionally the mass of an edifice was composed entirely of crude brick; but in such cases special precautions had to be taken to secure the stability of this comparatively frail material. In the first place, at intervals of four or five feet, a thick layer of reed matting was interposed along the whole extent of the building, which appears to have been intended to protect the earthy mass from disintegration, by its protection beyond the rest of the external surface. The readers of Herodotus are familiar with this feature, which (according to him) occurred in the massive walls whereby Babylon was surrounded. If this was really the case, we may conclude that those walls were not composed of burnt brick, as he imagined, but of the sun-dried material. Reeds were never employed in buildings composed of burnt brick, being useless in such cases; where their impression is found, as not unfrequently happens, on bricks of this kind, the brick has been laid upon reed matting when in a soft state, and afterwards submitted to the action of fire. In edifices of crude brick, the reeds were no doubt of great service, and have enabled some buildings of the kind to endure to the present day. They are very strikingly conspicuous where they occur, since they stripe the whole building with continuous horizontal lines, having at a distance somewhat the effect of the courses of dark marble in an Italian structure of the Byzantine period.

Another characteristic of the edifices in which crude brick is thus largely employed, is the addition externally of solid and massive buttresses of the burnt material. These buttresses have sometimes a very considerable projection; they are broad, but not high, extending less than half way up the walls against which they are placed.

Plate VIII.   Vol I.

Fig. 1.

Bowariyeh.

Fig. 2.

Mugheir Temple.

PLATE VIII

Two kinds of cement are used in the early structures. One is a coarse clay or mud, which is sometimes mixed with chopped straw; the other is bitumen. This last is of an excellent quality, and the bricks which it unites adhere often so firmly together that they can with difficulty be separated. As a gen eral rule, in the early buildings, the crude brick is laid in mud, while the bitumen is used to cement together the burnt bricks.

These general remarks will receive their best illustration from a detailed description of the principal early edifices which recent researches in Lower Mesopotamia have revealed to us. These are for the most part temples; but in one or two cases the edifice explored is thought to have been a residence, so that the domestic architecture of the period may be regarded as known to us, at least in some degree. The temples most carefully examined hitherto are those at Warka, Mugheir, and Abu-Shahrein, the first of which was explored by Mr. Loftus in 1854, the second by Mr. Taylor in the same year, and the third by the same traveller in 1855. The Warka ruin is called by the natives Bowariyeh, which signifies "reed mats," in allusion to a peculiarity, already noticed, in its construction. [PLATE VIII., Fig. 1.] It is at once the most central and the loftiest ruin in the place. At first sight it appears to have been a cone or pyramid; but further examination proves that it was in reality a tower, 200 feet square at the base, built in two stories, the lower story being composed entirely of sun-dried bricks laid in mud, and protected at intervals of four or five feet by layers of reeds, while the upper one was composed of the same material, faced with burnt brick. Of the upper stage very little remains; and this little is of a later date than the inferior story, which bears marks of a very high antiquity. The sundried bricks whereof the lower story is composed are "rudely moulded of very incoherent earth, mixed with fragments of pottery and fresh-water shells," and vary in size and shape, being sometimes square, seven inches each way; sometimes oblong, nine inches by seven, and from three to three and a half inches thick. The whole present height of the building is estimated at 100 feet above the level of the plain. Its summit, except where some slight remains of the second story constitute an interruption, is "perfectly flat," and probably continues very much in the condition in which it was when the lower stage was first built. This stage, being built of crude brick, was necessarily weak; it is therefore supported by four massive buttresses of baked brick, each placed exactly in the centre of one of the sides, and carried to about one-third of the height. Each buttress is nineteen feet high, six feet one inch wide, and seven and a half feet in depth; and each is divided down the middle by a receding space, one foot nine inches in width. All the bricks composing the buttresses are inscribed, and are very firmly cemented together with bitumen, in thick layers. The buttresses were entirely hidden under the mass of rubbish which had fallen from the building, chiefly from the upper story, and only became apparent when Mr. Loftus made his excavations.

It is impossible to reconstruct the Bowariyeh ruin from the facts and measurements hitherto supplied to us even the height of the first story is at present uncertain; and we have no means of so much as conjecturing the height of the second. The exact emplacement of the second upon the first is also doubtful, while the original mode of access is undiscovered; and thus the plan of the building is in many respects still defective. We only know that it was a square; that it had two stories at the least; and that its entire height above the plain considerably exceeded 100 feet. The temple at Mugheir has been more accurately examined. [PLATE VIII., Fig. 2.] On a mound or platform of some size, raised about twenty feet above the level of the plain, there stands a rectangular edifice, consisting at present of two stories, both of them ruined in parts, and buried to a considerable extent in piles of rubbish composed of their debris. The angles of the building exactly face the four cardinal points. It is not a square, but a parallelogram, having two longer and two shorter sides. [PLATE IX., Fig. 1.] The longer sides front to the north-east and south-west respectively, and measure 198 feet; while the shorter sides, which face the north-west and south-east, measure 133 feet. The present height of the basement story is 27 feet; but, allowing for the concealment of the lower part by the rubbish, and the destruction of the upper part by the hand of time, we may presume that the original height was little, if at all, short of 40 feet. The interior of this story is built of crude or sun-dried bricks of small size, laid in bitumen; but it is faced through out with a wall, ten feet in thickness, composed of red kiln dried bricks, likewise cemented with bitumen. This external wall is at once strengthened and diversified to the eye by a number of shallow buttresses or pilasters in the same material; of these there are nine, including the corner ones, on the longer, and six on the shorter sides. The width of the buttresses is eight feet, and their projection a little more than a foot. The walls and buttresses alike slope inwards at an angle of nine degrees. On the north-eastern side of the building there is a staircase nine feet wide, with sides or balustrades three feet wide, which leads up from the platform to the top of the first story. It has also been conjectured that there was a second or grand staircase on the south-east face, equal in width to the second story of the building, and thus occupying nearly the whole breadth of the structure on that side. A number of narrow slits or air-holes are carried through the building from side to side; they penetrate alike the walls and buttresses, and must have tended to preserve the dryness of the structure. The second story is, like the first, a parallelogram, and not of very different proportions. Its longer sides measure 119 feet, and its shorter ones 75 feet at the base. Its emplacement upon the first story is exact as respects the angles, but not central as regards the four sides. While it is removed from the south-eastern edge a distance of 47 feet, from the northwestern it is distant only 30 feet. From the two remaining sides its distance is apparently about 28 feet. The present height of the second story, including the rubbish upon its top, is 19 feet; but we may reasonably suppose that the original height was much greater. The material of which its inner structure is composed, seems to be chiefly (or wholly) partially-burnt brick, of a light red color, laid in a cement composed of lime and ashes. This central mass is faced with kiln-dried bricks of large size and excellent quality, also laid, except on the north-west face, in lime mortar. No buttresses and no staircase are traceable on this story; though it is possible that on the south-east side the grand staircase may have run the whole height of both stories.

According to information received by Mr. Taylor from the Arabs of the vicinity, there existed, less than half a century ago, some remains of a third story, on the summit of the rubbish which now crowns the second. This building is described as a room or chamber, and was probably the actual shrine of the god in whose honor the whole structure was erected. Mr. Taylor discovered a number of bricks or tiles glazed with a blue enamel, and also a number of large copper nails, at such a height in the rubbish which covers up much of the second story, that he thinks they could only have come from this upper chamber. The analogy of later Babylonian buildings, as of the Birs-Nimrud and the temple of Belus at Babylon confirms this view, and makes it probable that the early Chaldaean temple was a building in three stages, of which the first and second were solid masses of brickwork, ascended by steps on the outside, while the third was a small house or chamber highly ornamented, containing the image and shrine of the god. [PLATE IX., Fig. 2.]

Fig. 1.

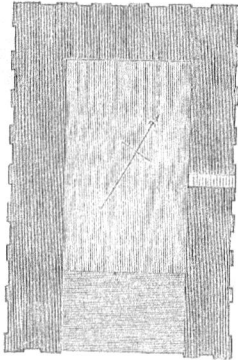

Ground-plan of Mugheir Temple.

Fig. 3.

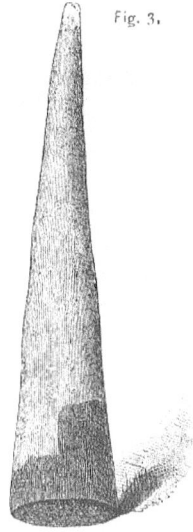

Terra cotta cone.   Actual size.

Fig 2.

Mugheir Temple restored.

PLATE IX

In conclusion, it must be observed that only the lower story of the Mugheir temple exhibits the workmanship of the old or Chaldaean period. Clay cylinders found in the upper story inform us that in its present condition this story is the work of Nabonidus, the last of the Babylonian kings; and most of its bricks bear his stamp. Some, however, have the stamp of the same monarch who built the lower story and this is sufficient to show that the two stories are a part of the original design, and therefore that the idea of building in stages belongs to the first kingdom and to primitive times. There is no evidence to prove whether the original edifice had, or had not, a third story; since the chamber seen by the Arabs was no doubt a late Babylonian work. The third story of the accompanying sketch must therefore be regarded as conjectural.

It is not necessary for our present purpose to detain the reader with a minute description of the ancient temple at Abu-Shahrein. The general character of this building seems to have very closely resembled that of the Mugheir temple. Its angles fronted the cardinal points: it had two stories, and an ornamented chamber at the top; it was faced with burnt brick, and strengthened by buttresses; and in most other respects followed the type of the Mugheir edifice. Its only very notable peculiarities are the partial use of stone in the construction, and the occurrence of a species of pillar, very curiously composed. The artificial platform on which the temple stands is made of beaten clay, cased with a massive wall of sandstone and limestone, in some places twenty feet thick. There is also a stone or rather marble, staircase which leads up from the platform to the summit of the first story, composed of small polished blocks, twenty-two inches long, thirteen broad, and four and a half thick. The bed of the staircase is made of sun dried brick, and the marble was fastened to this substratum by copper bolts, some portion of which was found by Mr. Taylor still adhering to the blocks. At the foot of the staircase there appear to have stood two columns, one on either side of it. The construction of these columns is very singular. A circular nucleus composed of sandstone slabs and small cylindrical pieces of marble disposed in alternate layers, was coated externally with coarse lime, mixed with small stones and pebbles, until by means of many successive layers the pillar had attained the desired bulk and thickness. Thus the stone and marble were entirely concealed under a thick coating of plaster; and a smoothness was given to the outer surface which it would have otherwise been difficult to obtain. The date of the Abu-Shahrein temple is thought to be considerably later than that of the other buildings above described; and the pillars would seem to be a refinement on the simplicity of the earlier times. The use of stone is to be accounted for, not so much by the advance of architectural science, as by the near vicinity of the Arabian hills, from which that material could be readily derived.

It is evident, that if the Chaldaean temples were of the character and construction which we have gathered from their remains, they could have possessed no great architectural beauty, though they may not have lacked a certain grandeur. In the dead level of Babylonia, an elevation even of 100 or 150 feet must have been impressive; and the plain massiveness of the structures no doubt added to their grand effect on the beholder. But there was singularly little in the buildings, architecturally viewed, to please the eye or gratify the sense of beauty. No edifices in the world—not even the Pyramids—are more deficient in external ornament. The buttresses and the air-holes, which alone break the flat uniformity of the walls, are intended simply for utility, and can scarcely be said to be much embellishment. If any efforts were made to delight by the ordinary resources of ornamental art, it seems clear that such efforts did not extend to the whole edifice, but were confined to the shrine itself—the actual abode of the god—the chamber which crowned the whole, and was alone, strictly speaking, "the temple." Even here there is no reason to believe that the building had externally much beauty. No fragments of architraves or capitals, no sculptured ornaments of any kind, have been found among the heaps of rubbish in which Chaldaean monuments are three-parts buried.

The ornaments which have been actually discovered, are such as suggest the idea of internal rather than external decoration; and they render it probable that such decoration was, at least in some cases, extremely rich. The copper nails and blue enamelled tiles found high up in the Mugheir mound, have been already noticed. At Abu-Shahrein the ground about the basement of the second story was covered with small pieces of agate, alabaster, and marble, finely cut and polished, from half an inch to two inches long, and half an inch (or somewhat less) in breadth, each with a hole drilled through its back, containing often a fragment of a copper bolt.

It was strewn less thickly with small plates of pure gold, and with a number of gold-headed or gilt, headed nails, used apparently to attach the gold plates to the internal plaster or wood-work. These fragments seem to attest the high ornamentation of the shrine in this instance, which we have no reason to regard is singular or in any way exceptional.

The Chaldaean remains which throw light upon the domestic architecture of the people are few and scanty. A small house was disinterred by Mr. Taylor at Mugheir, and the plan of some chambers was made out at Abu-Shahrein; but these are hitherto the only specimens which can be confidently assigned to the Chaldaean period. The house stood on a platform of sundried bricks, paved on the top with burnt bricks. It was built in the form of a cross, but with a good deal of irregularity, every wall being somewhat longer or shorter than the others. The material used in its construction was burnt brick, the outer layer imbedded in bitumen, and the remainder in a cement of mud. Externally the house was ornamented with perpendicular stepped recesses, while internally the bricks had often a thin coating of gypsum or enamel, upon which characters were inscribed. The floors of the chambers were paved with burnt brick, laid in bitumen. Two of the doorways were arched, the arch extending through the whole thickness of the walls; it was semicircular, and was constructed with bricks made wedge-shaped for the purpose. A good deal of charred date-wood was found in the house, probably the remains of rafters which had supported the roof.

The chambers at Abu-Shahrein were of sun-dried brick, with an internal covering of fine plaster, ornamented with paint. In one the ornamentation consisted of a series of red, black, and white bands, three inches in breadth; in another was represented, but very rudely, the figure of a man holding a bird on his wrist, with a smaller figure near him, in red paint. The favorite external ornamentation for houses seems to have been by means of colored cones in terra cotta, which were imbedded in moist mud or plaster, and arranged into a variety of patterns. [PLATE IX., Fig. 3.]

Plate X

Fig. 1.

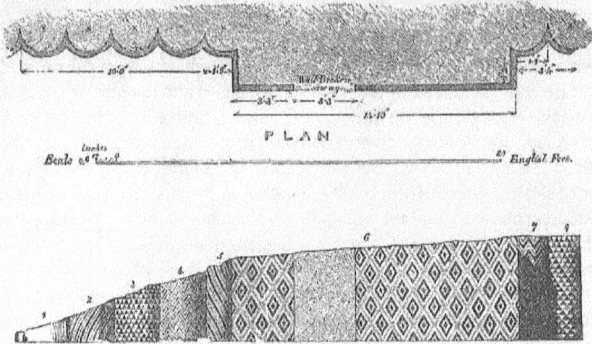

P L A N

Scale of Yards   20 English Feet.

1, 2, 3, 4, 5, 7, 8. Half-columns, patterned with coloured cones.
6, 7. Flat wall, projecting in front of the half-columns.

Fig. 2.

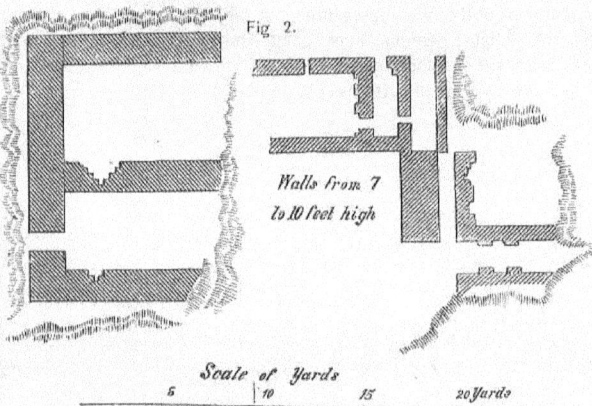

Walls from 7
to 10 feet high

Scale of Yards
5   10   15   20 Yards

Ground-plan of chambers excavated at Abu-Shahrein.

PLATE X

But little can be said as to the plan on which houses were built. [Illustration: PLATE X., Fig. 2.] The walls were generally of vast thickness, the chambers long and narrow, with the outer doors opening directly into them. The rooms ordinarily led into one another, passages being rarely found. Squared recesses, sometimes stepped or dentated, were common in the rooms; and in the arrangement of these something of symmetry is observable, as they frequently correspond to or face each other. The roofs were probably either flat-beams of palm-wood being stretched across from wall to wall—or else arched with brick. No indication of windows has been found as yet; but still it is thought that the chambers were lighted by them, only they were placed high, near the ceiling or roof, and thus do not appear in the existing ruins, which consists merely of the lower portion of walls, seldom exceeding the height of seven or eight feet. The doorways, both outer and inner, are towards the sides rather than in the centre of the apartments—a feature common to Chaldaean with Assyrian buildings.

Next to their edifices, the most remarkable of the remains which the Chaldaeans have left to after-ages, are their burial-places. While ancient tombs are of very rare occurrence in Assyria and Upper Babylonia, Chaldaea Proper abounds with them. It has been conjectured, with some show of reason, that the Assyrians, in the time of their power, may have made the sacred land of Chai the general depository of their dead, much in the same way as the Persians even now use Kerbela and Nedjif or Meshed Ali as special cemetery cities, to which thousands of corpses are brought annually. At any rate, the quantity of human relics accumulated upon certain Chaldaean sites is enormous, and seems to be quite beyond what the mere population of the surrounding district could furnish. At Warka, for instance, excepting the triangular space between the three principal ruins, the whole remainder of the platform, the whole space within the walls, and an unknown extent of desert beyond them, are everywhere filled with human bones and sepulchres. In places coffins are piled upon coffins, certainly to the depth of 30, probably to the depth of 60 feet; and for miles on every side of the ruins the traveller walks upon a soil teeming with the relics of ancient, and now probably extinct, races. Sometimes these relics manifestly belong to a number of distinct and widely separate eras; but there are places where it is otherwise. However we may account for it—and no account has been yet given which is altogether satisfactory—it seems clear, from the comparative homogeneousness of the remains in some places, that they belong to a single race, and if not to a single period, at any rate to only two, or, at the most, three distinct periods, so that it is no longer very difficult to distinguish the more ancient from the later relics. Such is the character of the remains at Mugheir, which are thought to contain nothing of later date than the close of the Babylonian period, B. C. 538; and such is, still more remarkably, the character of the ruins at Abu-Shahrein and Tel-el-Lahm, which seem to be entirely, or almost entirely, Chaldaean. In the following account of the coffins and mode of burial employed by the early Chaldaeans, examples will be drawn from these places only; since otherwise we should be liable to confound together the productions of very different ages and peoples.

Plate. XI.

Fig. 1.

Brick vault at Mugheir.

Fig. 2.

No. 1.

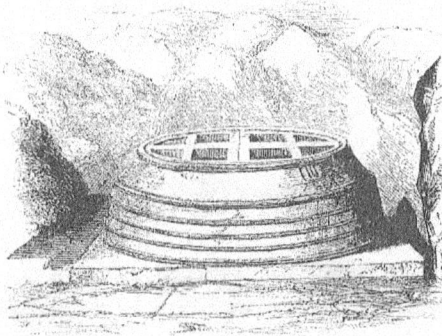

PLATE XI

The tombs to which an archaic character most certainly attaches are of three kinds-brick vaults, clay coffins shaped like a dish-cover, and coffins in the same material, formed of two large jars placed mouth to mouth, and cemented together with bitumen. The brick vaults are found chiefly at Mugheir. [PLATE XI., Fig. 1.] They are seven feet long, three feet seven inches broad, and five feet high, composed of sun-dried bricks imbedded in mud, and exhibit a very remarkable form and construction of the arch. The side walls of the vaults slope outwards as they ascend; and the arch is formed, like those in Egyptian buildings and Scythian tombs, by each successive layer of bricks, from the point where the arch begins, a little overlapping the last, till the two sides of the roof are brought so near together that the aperture may be closed by a single brick. The floor of the vaults was paved with brick similar to that used for the roof and sides; on this floor was commonly spread a matting of reeds, and the body was laid upon the matting. It was commonly turned on its left side, the right arm falling towards the left, and the fingers resting on the edge of a copper bowl, usually placed on the palm of the left hand. The head was pillowed on a single sun-dried brick. Various articles of ornament and use were interred with each body, which will be more particularly described hereafter. Food seems often to have been placed in the tombs, and jars or other drinking vessels are universal. The brick vaults appear to have been family sepulchres; they have often received three or four bodies, and in one case a single vault contained eleven skeletons.

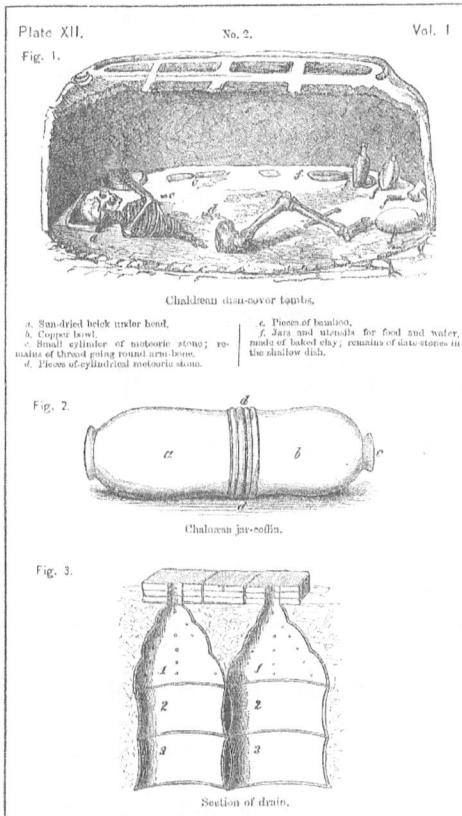

Plate XII.   No. 2.   Vol. I

Fig. 1.

Chaldæan dish-cover tombs.

a. Sun-dried brick under head.
b. Copper bowl.
c. Small cylinder of meteoric stone; remains of thread going round arm-bone.
d. Pieces of cylindrical meteoric stone.

e. Pieces of bamboo.
f. Jars and utensils for food and water, made of baked clay; remains of date-stones in the shallow dish.

Fig. 2.

Chaldæan jar-coffin.

Fig. 3.

Section of drain.

PLATE XII

The clay coffins, shaped like a dish-cover, are among the most curious of the sepulchral remains of antiquity. [PLATE XI., Fig. 2; PLATE XII., Fig. 1.] On a platform of sun-dried brick is laid a mat exactly similar to those in common use among the Arabs of the country at the present day; and hereon lies the skeleton disposed as in the brick vaults, and surrounded by utensils and ornaments. Mat, skeleton, and utensils are then concealed by a huge cover in burnt clay, formed of a single piece, which is commonly seven feet long, two or three feet high, and two feet and a half broad at the bottom. It is rarely that modern potters produce articles of half the size. Externally the covers have commonly some slight ornament, such as rims and shallow indentations, as represented in the sketch (No. 1). Internally they are plain. Not more than two skeletons have ever been found under a single cover; and in these cases they were the skeletons of a male and a female. Children were interred separately, under covers about half the size of those for adults. Tombs of this kind commonly occur at some considerable depth. None were discovered at Mugheir nearer the surface than seven or eight feet.

The third kind of tomb, common both at Mugheir and at Telel-Lahm, is almost as eccentric as the preceding. Two large open-mouthed jars (a and b), shaped like the largest of the water-jars at present in use at Baghdad, are taken, and the body is disposed inside them with the usual accompaniments of dishes, vases, and ornaments. [PLATE XII. Fig. 2.] The jars average from two and a half feet to three feet in depth, and have a diameter of about two feet; so that they would readily contain a full-sized corpse if it was slightly bent at the knees.

Sometimes the two jars are of equal size, and are simply united at their mouths by a layer of bitumen (dd); but more commonly one is slightly larger than the other, and the smaller mouth is inserted into the larger one for a depth of three or four inches, while a coating of bitumen is still applied externally at the juncture. In each coffin there is an air-hole at one extremity (c) to allow the escape of the gases generated during decomposition.

Besides the coffins themselves, some other curious features are found in the burial-places. The dead are commonly buried, not underneath the natural surface of the ground, but in extensive artificial mounds, each mound containing a vast number of coffins. The coffins are arranged side by side, often in several layers; and occasionally strips of masonry, crossing each other at right angles, separate the sets of coffins from their neighbors. The surface of the mounds is sometimes paved with brick; and a similar pavement often separates the layers of coffins one from another. But the most remarkable feature in the tomb-mounds is their system of drainage. Long shafts of baked clay extend from the surface of the mound to its base, composed of a succession of rings two feet in diameter, and about a foot and a half in breadth, joined together by thin layers of bitumen. [PLATE XII., Fig. 3.] To give the rings additional strength, the sides have a slight concave curve and, still further to resist external pressure, the shafts are filled from bottom to top with a loose mass of broken pottery. At the top the shaft contracts rapidly by means of a ring of a peculiar shape, and above this ring are a series of perforated bricks leading up to the top of the mound, the surface of which is so arranged as to conduct the rain-water into these orifices. For the still more effectual drainage of the mound, the top-piece of the shaft immediately below the perforated bricks, and also the first rings, are full of small holes to admit any stray moisture; and besides this, for the space of a foot every way, the shafts are surrounded with broken pottery, so that the real diameter of each drain is as much as four feet. By these arrangements the piles have been kept perfectly dry; and the consequence is the preservation, to the present day, not only of the utensils and ornaments placed in the tombs, but of the very skeletons themselves, which are seen perfect on opening a tomb, though they generally crumble to dust at the first touch.

The skill of the Chaldaeans as potters has received considerable illustration in the foregoing pages. No ordinary ingenuity was needed to model and bake the large vases, and still larger covers, which were the ordinary receptacles of the Chaldaean dead. The rings and top-pieces of the drainage-shafts also exhibit much skill and knowledge of principles. Hitherto, however, the reader has not been brought into contact with any specimens of Chaldaean fictile art which can be regarded as exhibiting elegance of form, or, indeed, any sense of beauty as distinguished from utility. Such specimens are, in fact, somewhat scarce, but they are not wholly wanting. Among the vases and drinking vessels with which the Chaldaean tombs abound, while the majority are characterized by a certain rudeness both of shape and material, we occasionally meet with specimens of a higher character, which would not shrink from a comparison with the ordinary productions of Greek fictile art. A number of these are represented in the second figure [PLATE XIII., Fig 2], which exhibits several forms not hitherto published-some taken from drawings by Mr. Churchill, the artist who accompanied Mr. Loftus on his first journey; others drawn for the present work from vases now in the British Museum.

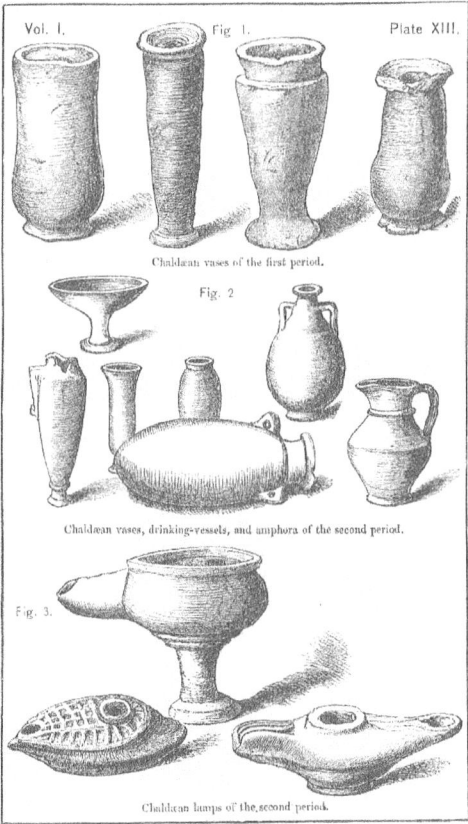

Vol. I.   Fig. 1.   Plate XIII.

Chaldæan vases of the first period.

Fig. 2

Chaldæan vases, drinking-vessels, and amphora of the second period.

Fig. 3.

Chaldæan lamps of the second period.

PLATE XIII

It is evident that, while the vases of the first group are roughly moulded by the hand, the vases and lamps of the second have been carefully shaped by the aid of the potter's wheel. These last are formed of a far finer clay than the early specimens, and have sometimes a slight glaze upon them, which adds much to their beauty.

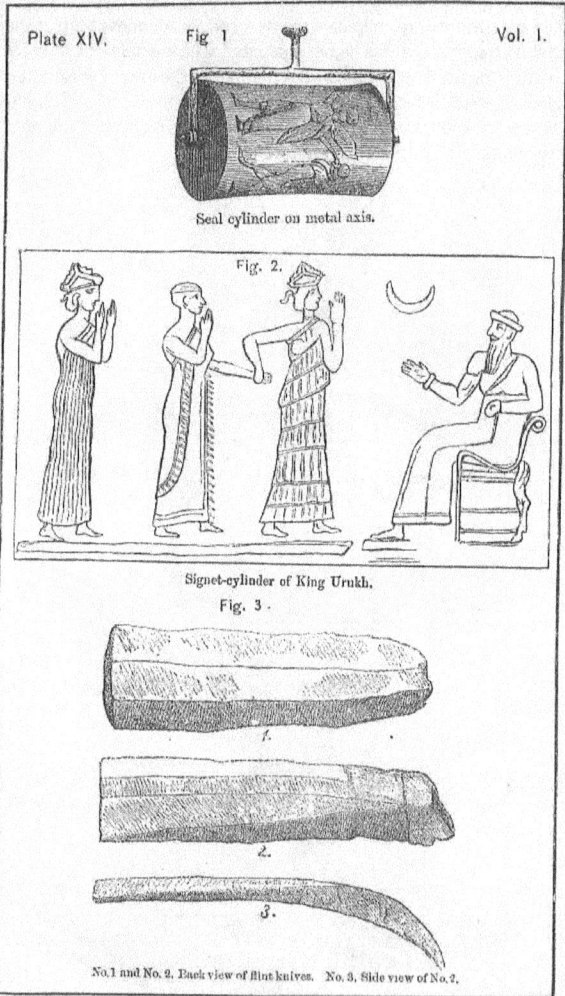

Plate XIV.   Fig 1   Vol. I.

Seal cylinder on metal axis.

Fig. 2.

Signet-cylinder of King Urukh.

Fig. 3.

No.1 and No. 2, Back view of flint knives.   No. 3, Side view of No. 2.

PLATE XIV

In a few instances the works of the Chaldaeans in this material belong to mimetic art, of which they are rude but interesting specimens. Some of the primitive graves at Senkareh yielded tablets of baked clay, on which were represented, in low relief, sometimes single figures of men, sometimes groups, sometimes men in combination with animals. A scene in which a lion is disturbed in its feast off a bullock, by a man armed with a club and a mace or hatchet, possesses remarkable spirit, and, were it not for the strange drawing of the lion's unlifted leg, might be regarded as a very creditable performance. In another, a lion is represented devouring a prostrate human being; while a third exhibits a pugilistic encounter after the most approved fashion of modern England. It is perhaps uncertain whether these tablets belong to the Chaldaean or to the Babylonian period, but on the whole their rudeness and simplicity favor the earlier rather than the later date.

The only other works having anything of an artistic character, that can be distinctly assigned to the primitive period, are a certain number of engraved cylinders, some of which are very curious. [PLATE XIV., Fig. 1] It is clearly established that the cylinders in question, which are generally of serpentine, meteoric stone, jasper, chalcedony, or other similar substance, were the seals or signets of their possessors, who impressed them upon the moist clay which formed the ordinary material for writing. They are round, or nearly so, and measure from half an inch to three inches in length; ordinarily they are about one-third of their length in diameter. A hole is bored through the stone from end to end, so that it could be worn upon a string; and cylinders are found in some of the earliest tombs which have been worn round the wrist in this way. In early times they may have been impressed by the hand; but afterwards it was common to place them upon a bronze or copper axis attached to a handle, by means of which they were rolled across the clay from one end to the other. The cylinders are frequently unengraved, and this is most commonly their condition in the primitive tombs; out there is some very curious evidence, from which it appears that the art of engraving them was really known and practised (though doubtless in rare instances) at a very early date. The signet cylinder of the monarch who founded the most ancient of the buildings at Mugheir, Warka, Senkareh, and Niffer, and who thus stands at the head of the monumental kings, was in the possession of Sir R. Porter; and though it is now lost, an engraving made from it is preserved in his "Travels." [PLATE XIV., Fig. 2.] The signet cylinder of this monarch's son has been recently recovered, and is now in the British Museum. We are entitled to conclude from the data thus in our possession that the art of cylinder-engraving had, even at this early period, made considerable progress. The letters of the inscriptions, which give the names of the kings and their titles, are indeed somewhat rudely formed, as they are on the stamped bricks of the period; but the figures have been as well cut, and as flowingly traced, as those of a later date. It was thought possible that the artist employed by Sir R. Porter had given a flattering representation of his original, but the newly recovered relic, known as the "cylinder of Ilgi," bears upon it figures of quite as great excellence: and we are thus led to the conclusion that both mechanical and artistic skill had reached a very surprising degree of excellence at the most remote period to which the Chaldaean records carry us back.

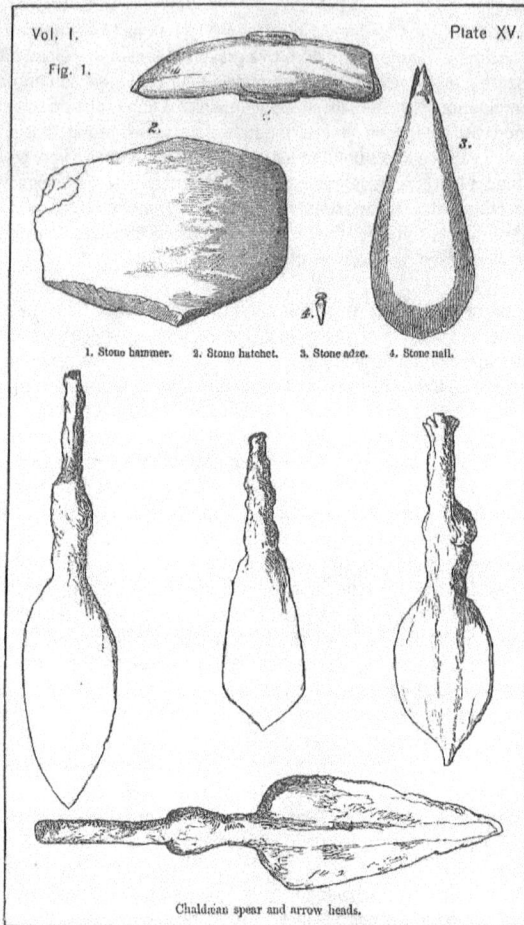

Fig. 1.

1. Stone hammer.   2. Stone hatchet.   3. Stone adze.   4. Stone nail.

Chaldæan spear and arrow heads.

PLATE XV

It increases the surprise which we naturally feel at the discovery of these relics to reflect upon the rudeness of the implements with which such results would seem to have been accomplished. In the primitive Chaldaean ruins, the implements which have been discovered are either in stone or bronze. Iron in the early times is seemingly unknown, and when it first appears is wrought into ornaments for the person. Knives of flint or chert [PLATE XIV., Fig. 3], stone hatchets, hammers, adzes, and nails, are common in the most ancient mounds, which contain also a number of clay models, the centres, as it is thought, of moulds into which molten bronze was run, and also occasionally the bronze instruments themselves, as (in addition to spear heads and arrow-heads) hammers, adzes, hatchets, knives, and sickles. It will be seen by the engraved representations that these instruments are one and all of a rude and coarse character. [PLATE XV.], [PLATE XVI.] The flint and stone knives, axes, and hammers, which abound in all the true Chaldaean mounds, are somewhat more advanced indeed than those very primitive implements which have been found in a drift; but they are of a workmanship at least as unskilled as that of the ordinary stone celts of Western and Northern Europe, which till the discoveries of M. Perthes were regarded as the most ancient human remains in our quarter of the globe. They indicate some practical knowledge of the cleavage of silicious rocks, but they show no power of producing even such finish as the celts frequently exhibit. In one case only has a flint instrument been discovered perfectly regular in form, and presenting a sharp angular exactness. The instrument, which is figured [PLATE XVI., Fig. 2], is a sort of long parallelogram, round at the back, and with a deep impression down its face. Its use is uncertain; but, according to a reasonable conjecture, it may have been designed for impressing characters upon the moist clay of tablets and cylinders—a purpose for which it is said to be excellently fitted.

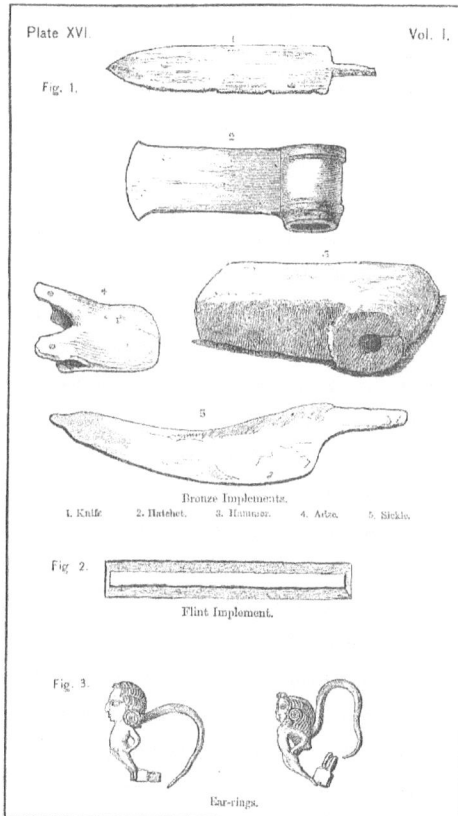

PLATE XVI

The metallurgy of the Chaldaeans, though indicative of a higher state of civilization and a greater knowledge of the useful arts than their stone weapons, is still of a somewhat rude character, and indicates a nation but just emerging out of an almost barbaric simplicity. Metal seems to be scarce, and not many kinds are found. There is no silver, zinc, or platinum; but only gold, copper, tin, lead, and iron. Gold is found in beads, ear-rings, and other ornaments, which are in some instances of a fashion that is not inelegant. [PLATE XVI., Fig. 3.] Copper occurs pure, but is more often hardened by means of an alloy of tin, whereby it becomes bronze, and is rendered suitable for implements and weapons. Lead is rare, occurring only in a very few specimens, as in one jar or bottle, and in what seems to be a portion of a pipe, brought by Mr. Loftus from Mugheir. [PLATE XVII., Fig. 1.] Iron, as already observed, is extremely uncommon; and when it occurs, is chiefly used for the rings and bangles which seem to have been among the favorite adornments of the people. Bronze is, however, even for these, the more common material. [PLATE XVII, Fig. 2.] It is sometimes wrought into thin and elegant shapes, tapering to a point at either extremity; sometimes the form into which it is cast is coarse and massive, resembling a solid bar twisted into a rude circle. For all ordinary purposes of utility it is the common metal used. A bronze or copper bowl is found in almost every tomb; bronze bolts remain in the pieces of marble used for tesselating; bronze rings sometimes strengthen the cones used for ornamenting walls; bronze weapons and instruments are, as we have seen, common, and in the same material have been found chains, nails, toe and finger rings, armlets, bracelets, and fish-hooks.

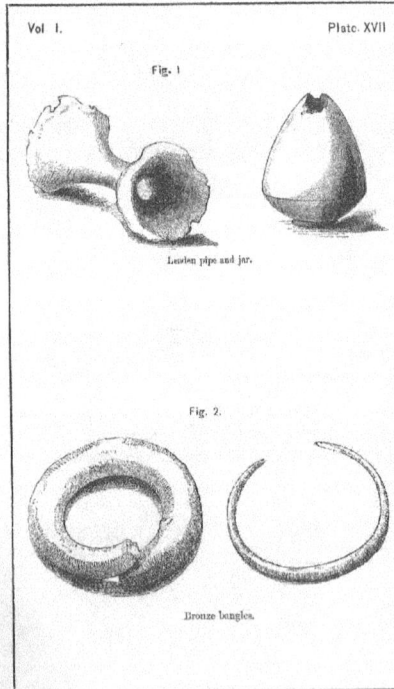

Vol I.   Plate XVII

Fig. 1

Leaden pipe and jar.

Fig. 2.

Bronze bangles.

PLATE XVII

No long or detailed account can be given of the textile fabrics of the ancient Chaldaeans; but there is reason to believe that this was a branch of industry in which they particularly excelled. We know that as early as the time of Joshua a Babylonian garment had been imported into Palestine, and was of so rare a beauty as to attract the covetous regards of Achan, in common with certain large masses of the precious metals. The very ancient cylinder figured above must belong to a time at least five or six centuries earlier; upon it we observe flounced and fringed garments, delicately striped, and indicative apparently of an advanced state of textile manufacture. Recent researches do not throw much light on this subject. The frail materials of which human apparel is composed can only under peculiar circumstances resist the destructive power of thirty or forty centuries; and consequently we have but few traces of the actual fabrics in use among the primitive people. Pieces of linen are said to have been found attaching to some of the skeletons in the tombs; and the sun-dried brick which supports the head is sometimes covered with the remains of a "tasselled cushion of tapestry;" but otherwise we are without direct evidence either as to the material in use, or as to the character of the fabric. In later times Babylon was especially celebrated for its robes and its carpets. Such evidence as we have would seem to make it probable that both manufactures had attained to considerable excellence in Chaldaean times.

The only sciences in which the early Chaldaeans can at present be proved to have excelled are the cognate ones of arithmetic and astronomy. On the broad and monotonous plains of Lower Mesopotamia, where the earth has little upon it to suggest thought or please by variety, the "variegated heaven," ever changing with the hours and with the seasons, would early attract attention, while the clear sky, dry atmosphere, and level horizon would afford facilities for observations, so soon as the idea of them suggested itself to the minds of the inhabitants. The "Chaldaean learning" of a later age appears to have been originated, in all its branches, by the primitive people; in whose language it continued to be written even in Semitic times.

We are informed by Simplicius that Callisthenes, who accompanied Alexander to Babylon, sent to Aristotle from that capital a series of astronomical observations, which he had found preserved there, extending back to a period of 1903 years from Alexander's conquest of the city. Epigenes related that these observations were recorded upon tablets of baked clay, which is quite in accordance with all that we know of the literary habits of the people. They must have extended, according to Simplicius, as far back as B.C. 2234, and would therefore seem to have been commenced and carried on for many centuries by the primitive Chaldaean people. We have no means of determining their exact nature or value, as none of them have been preserved to us: no doubt they were at first extremely simple; but we have every reason to conclude that they were of a real and substantial character. There is nothing fanciful, or (so to speak) astrological, in the early astronomy of the Babylonians. Their careful emplacement of their chief buildings, which were probably used from the earliest times for astronomical purposes, their invention of different kinds of dials, and their division of the day into those hours which we still use, are all solid, though not perhaps very brilliant, achievements. It was only in later times that the Chaldaeans were fairly taxed with imposture and charlatanism; in early ages they seem to have really deserved the eulogy bestowed on them by Cicero.

It may have been the astronomical knowledge of the Chaldaeans which gave them the confidence to adventure on important voyages. Scripture tells us of the later people, that "their cry was in the ships;" and the early inscriptions not only make frequent mention of the "ships of Ur," but by connecting these vessels with those of Ethiopia seem to imply that they were navigated to considerable distances. Unfortunately we possess no materials from which to form any idea either of the make and character of the Chaldaean vessels, or of the nature of the trade in which they were employed. We may perhaps assume that at first they were either canoes hollowed out of a palm-trunk, or reed fabrics made water-tight by a coating of bitumen. The Chaldaea trading operations lay no doubt, chiefly in the Persian Gulf; but it is quite possible that even in very early times they were not confined to this sheltered basin. The gold, which was so lavishly used in decoration, could only have been obtained in the necessary quantities from Africa or India; and it is therefore probable that one, if not both, of these countries was visited by the Chaldaean traders.

Astronomical investigations could not be conducted without a fair proficiency in the science of numbers. It would be reasonable to conclude, from the admitted character of the Chaldaeans as astronomers, that they were familiar with most arithmetical processes, even had we no evidence upon the subject. Evidence, however, to a certain extent, does exist. On a tablet found at Senkareh, and belonging probably to an early period, a table of squares is given, correctly calculated from one to sixty. The system of notation, which is here used, is very curious. Berosus informs us that, in their computations of time, the Chaldaeans employed an alternate sexagesimal and decimal notation, reckoning the years by the soss, the ner, and the sar—the soss being a term of 60 years, the ner one of 600, and the sar one of 3600 (or 60 sosses). It appears from the Senkareh monument, that they occasionally pursued the same practice in mere numerical calculations, as will be evident from the illustration. [PLATE XVIII., Figs. 1, 2.]

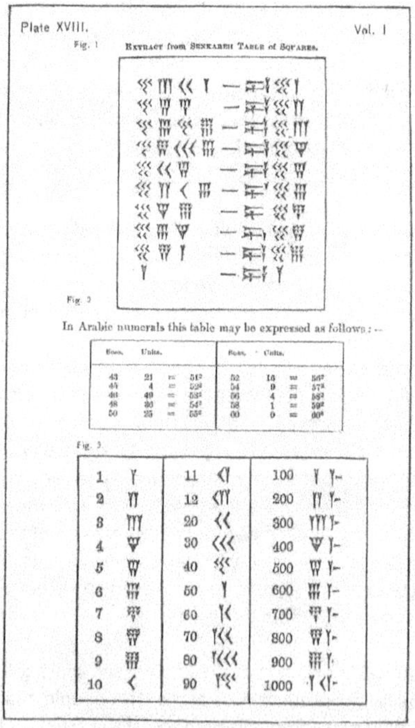

PLATE XVIII

In Arabic numerals this table may be expressed as follows:

Soss.	Units.			Soss.	Units.		
43	21	$=$	51^2	52	16	$=$	56^2
45	4	$=$	52^2	54	9	$=$	57^2
46	49	$=$	53^2	56	4	$=$	58^2
48	36	$=$	54^2	58	1	$=$	59^2
50	25	$=$	55^2	60	0	$=$	60^2

The calculation is in every case correct; and the notation is by means of two signs—the simple wedge ⟆, and the arrow-head ◄; the wedge representing the unit, the soss (60), and the sar (3600), while the arrowhead expresses the decades of each series, or the numbers 10 and 600.[91]

The notation is cumbrous, but scarcely more so than that of the Romans. It would be awkward to use, from the paucity in the number of signs, which could scarcely fail to give rise to confusion,—more especially as it does not appear that there was any way of expressing a cipher. It is not probable that at any time it was the notation in ordinary use. Numbers were commonly expressed in a manner not unlike the Roman, as will be seen by the subjoined table. [PLATE XVIII., Fig. 3.] One, ten, a hundred, and a thousand, had distinct signs. Fifty had the same sign as the unit—a simple wedge. The other numbers were composed from these elements.

CHAPTER VI

MANNERS AND CUSTOMS

Chaldaea, unlike Egypt, has preserved to our day but few records of the private or domestic life of its inhabitants. Beyond the funereal customs, to which reference was made in the last chapter, we can obtain from the monuments but a very scanty account of their general mode of life, manners, and usages. Some attempt, however, must be made to throw together the few points of this nature on which we have obtained any light from recent researches in Mesopotamia.

The ordinary dress of the common people among the Chaldaeans seems to have consisted of a single garment, a short tunic, tied round the waist, and reaching thence to the knees, a costume very similar to that worn by the Madan Arabs at the present day. To this may sometimes have been added an abba, or cloak, thrown over the shoulders, and falling below the tunic, about half-way down the calf of the leg. The material of the former we may perhaps presume to have been linen, which best suits the climate, and is a fabric found in the ancient tombs. The outer cloak was most likely of woollen, and served to protect hunters and others against the occasional inclemency of the air. The feet were unprotected by either shoes or sandals; on the head was worn a skull-cap, or else a band of camel's hairs—the germ of the turban which has now become universal throughout the East.

The costume of the richer class was more elaborate. A high mitre, of a very peculiar appearance, or else a low cap ornamented with two curved horns, covered the head. [PLATE XIX. Fig. 1.] The neck and arms were bare. The chief garment was a long gown or robe, extending from the neck to the feet, commonly either striped or flounced, or both; and sometimes also adorned with fringe. This robe, which was scanty according to modern notions, appears not to have been fastened by any girdle or cincture round the waist, but to have been kept in place by passing over one shoulder, a slit or hole being made for the arm on one side of the dress only. In some cases the upper part of the dress seems to have been detached from the lower, and to have formed a sort of jacket, which reached about to the hips.

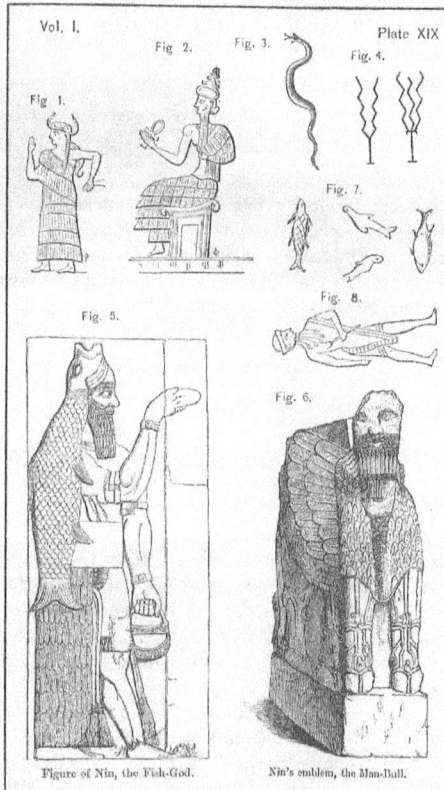

PLATE XIX

The beard was commonly worn straight and long, not in crisp curls, as by the Assyrians. [PLATE XIX., Fig. 2.] The hair was also worn long, either gathered together into a club behind the head, or depending in long spiral curls on either side the face and down the back. Ornaments were much affected, especially by the women. Bronze and iron bangles and armlets, and bracelets of rings or beads, ear-rings, and rings for the toes, are common in the tombs, and few female skeletons are without them. The material of the ornaments is generally of small value. Many of the rings are formed by grinding down a small kind of shell; the others are of bronze or iron. Agate beads, however, are not uncommon, and gold beads have been found in a few tombs, as well as some other small ornaments in the same material. The men seem to have carried generally an engraved cylinder in agate or other hard stone, which was used as a seal or signet, and was probably worn round the wrist. Sometimes rings, and even bracelets, formed also a part of their adornment. The latter were occasionally in gold—they consisted of bands or fillets of the pure beaten metal, and were as much as an inch in breadth.

The food of the early Chaldaeans consisted probably of the various esculents which have already been mentioned as products of the territory. The chief support, however, of the mass of the population was, beyond a doubt, the dates, which still form the main sustenance of those who inhabit the country. It is clear that in Babylonia, as in Scythia, the practice existed of burying with a man a quantity of the food to which he had been accustomed during life. In the Chaldaean sepulchres a number of dishes are always ranged round the skeleton, containing the viaticum of the deceased person, and in these dishes are almost invariably found a number of date-stones. They are most commonly unaccompanied by any traces of other kinds of food; occasionally, however, besides date-stones, the bones of fish and of chickens have been discovered, from which we may conclude that those animals were eaten, at any rate by the upper classes. Herodotus tells us that in his day three tribes of Babylonians subsisted on fish alone; and the present inhabitants of Lower Mesopotamia make it a principal article of their diet. The rivers and the marshes produce it in great abundance, while the sea is also at hand, if the fresh-water supply should fail. Carp and barbel are the principal fresh-water sorts, and of these the former grows to a very great size in the Euphrates. An early tablet, now in the British Museum, represents a man carrying a large fish by the head, which may be a carp, though the species can scarcely be identified. There is evidence that the wild-boar was also eaten by the primitive people; for Mr. Loftus found a jaw of this animal, with the tusk still remaining, lying in a shallow clay dish in one of the tombs. Perhaps we may be justified in concluding, from the comparative rarity of any remains of animal food in the early sepulchres, that the primitive Chaldaeans subsisted chiefly on vegetable productions. The variety and excellence of such esculents are prominently put forward by Berosus in his account of the original condition of the country; and they still form the principal support of those who now inhabit it.

We are told that Nimrod was "a mighty hunter before the Lord;" and it is evident, from the account already given of the animals indigenous in Lower Mesopotainia, that there was abundant room for the display of a sportsman's skill and daring when men first settled in that region. The Senkareh tablets show the boldness and voracity of the Chaldaean lion, which not only levied contributions on the settlers' cattle, but occasionally ventured to attack man himself. We have not as yet any hunting scenes belonging to these early times; but there can be little doubt that the bow was the chief weapon used against the king of beasts, whose assailants commonly prefer remaining at a respectful distance from him. The wild-boar may have been hunted in the same way, or he may have been attacked with a spear—a weapon equally well known with the bow to the early settlers. Fish were certainly taken with the hook; for fish-hooks have been found in the tombs; but probably they were also captured in nets, which are among the earliest of human inventions.

A considerable portion of the primitive population must have been engaged in maritime pursuits. In the earliest inscriptions we find constant mention of the "ships of Ur," which appear to have traded with Ethiopia —a country whence may have been derived the gold, which—as has been already shown—was so largely used by the Chaldaeans in ornamentation. It would be interesting could we regard it as proved that they traded also with the Indian peninsula; but the "rough logs of wood, apparently teak," which Mr. Taylor discovered in the great temple at Mugheir, belong more probably to the time of its repair by Nabonidus than to that of its original construction by a Chaldaean monarch. The Sea-God was one of the chief objects of veneration at Ur and elsewhere; and Berosus appears to have preserved an authentic tradition, where he makes the primitive people of the country derive their arts and civilization from "the Red Sea." Even if their commercial dealings did not bring them into contact with any more advanced people, they must have increased the intelligence, as well as the material resources, of those employed in them, and so have advanced their civilization.

Such are the few conclusions concerning the manners of the Chaldaeans which alone we seem to have any right to form with our present means of information.

CHAPTER VII

RELIGION

The religion of the Chaldaeans, from the very earliest times to which the monuments carry us back, was, in its outward aspect, a polytheism of a very elaborate character. It is quite possible that there may have been esoteric explanations, known to the priests and the more learned, which, resolving the personages of the Pantheon into the powers of nature, reconciled the apparent multiplicity of gods with monotheism, or even with atheism. So far, however, as outward appearances were concerned, the worship was grossly polytheistic. Various deities, whom it was not considered at all necessary to trace to a single stock, divided the allegiance of the people, and even of the kings, who regarded with equal respect, and glorified with equally exalted epithets, some fifteen or sixteen personages. Next to these principal gods were a far more numerous assemblage of inferior or secondary divinities, less often mentioned, and regarded as less worthy of honor, but still recognized generally through the country. Finally, the Pantheon contained a host of mere local gods or genii, every town and almost every village in Babylonia being under the protection of its own particular divinity.

It will be impossible to give a complete account of this vast and complicated system. The subject is still but partially worked out by cuneiform scholars; the difficulties in the way of understanding it are great; and in many portions to which special attention has been paid it is strangely perplexing and bewildering. All that will be attempted in the present place is to convey an idea of the general character of the Chaldaean religion, and to give some information with regard to the principal deities.

In the first place, it must be noticed that the religion was to a certain extent astral. The heaven itself, the sun, the moon, and the five planets, have each their representative in the Chaldaean Pantheon among the chief objects of worship. At the same time it is to be observed that the astral element is not universal, but partial; and that, even where it has place, it is but one aspect of the mythology, not by any means its full and complete exposition. The Chaldaean religion even here is far from being mere Sabaeanism—the simple worship of the "host of heaven." The aether, the sun, the moon, and still more the five planetary gods, are something above and beyond those parts of nature. Like the classical Apollo and Diana, Mars and Venus, they are real persons, with a life and a history, a power and an influence, which no ingenuity can translate into a metaphorical representation of phenomena attaching to the air and to the heavenly bodies. It is doubtful, indeed, whether the gods of this class are really of astronomical origin, and not rather primitive deities, whose character and attributes were, to a great extent, fixed and settled before the notion arose of connecting them with certain parts of nature. Occasionally they seem to represent heroes rather than celestial bodies; and they have all attributes quite distinct from their physical or astronomical character.

Secondly, the striking resemblance of the Chaldaean system to that of the Classical Mythology seems worthy of particular attention. This resemblance is too general, and too close in some respects, to allow of the supposition that mere accident has produced the coincidence. In the Pantheons of Greece and Rome, and in that of Chaldaea, the same general grouping is to be recognized; the same genealogical succession is not unfrequently to be traced; and in some cases even the familiar names and titles of classical divinities admit of the most curious illustration and explanation from Chaldaean sources. We can scarcely doubt but that, in some way or other, there was a communication of beliefs—a passage in very early times, from the shores of the Persian Gulf to the lands washed by the Mediterranean, of mythological notions and ideas. It is a probable conjecture that among the primitive tribes who dwelt on the Tigris and Euphrates, when the cuneiform alphabet was invented and when such writing was first applied to the purposes of religion, a Scythic or Scytho-Arian race existed, who subsequently migrated to Europe, and brought with them those mythical traditions which, as objects of popular belief, had been mixed up in the nascent literature of their native country, and that these traditions were passed on to the classical nations, who were in part descended from this Scythic or Scytho-Arian people.

The grouping of the principal Chalda an deities is as follows. At the head of the Pantheon stands a god, Il or Ra, of whom but little is known. Next to him is a Triad, Ana, Bil or Belus, and Hea or Hoa, who correspond closely to the classical Pluto, Jupiter, and Neptune. Each of these is accompanied by a female principle or wife, Ana by Anat, Bil (or Bel) by Mulita or Beltis, and Hea (or Hoa) by Davkina. Then follows a further Triad, consisting of Sin or Hurki, the Moon-god; San or Sansi, the Sun; and Vul the god of the atmosphere. The members of this Triad are again accompanied by female powers or wives,—Vul by a goddess called Shala or Tala, San (the Sun) by Gula or Anunit, and Hurki (the Moon) by a goddess whose name is wholly uncertain, but whose common title is "the great lady."

Such are the gods at the head of the Pantheon. Next in order to them we find a group of five minor deities, the representatives of the five planets,—Nin or Ninip (Saturn), Merodach (Jupiter), Nergal (Mars), Ishtar (Venus), and Nebo (Mercury). These together constitute what we have called the principal gods; after them are to be placed the numerous divinities of the second and third order.

These principal gods do not appear to have been connected, like the Egyptian and the classical divinities, into a single genealogical scheme: yet still a certain amount of relationship was considered to exist among them. Ana and Bel, for instance, were brothers, the sons of Il or Ra; Vul was son of Ana; Hurki, the Moon-god, of Bel; Nebo and Merodach were sons of Hea or Hoa. Many deities, however, are without parentage, as not only Il or Ra, but Hea, San (the Sun), Ishtar, and Nergal. Sometimes the relationship alleged is confused, and even contradictory, as in the case of Nin or Ninip, who is at one time the son, at another the father of Bel, and who is at once the son and the husband of Beltis. It is evident that the genealogical aspect is not that upon which much stress is intended to be laid, or which is looked upon as having much reality. The great gods are viewed habitually rather as a hierarchy of coequal powers, than as united by ties implying on the one hand pre-eminence and on the other subordination.

We may now consider briefly the characters and attributes of the several deities so far as they can be made out, either from the native records, or from classical tradition. And, first, concerning the god who stands in some sense at the head of the Chaldaean Pantheon.

IL, or RA.

The form Ra represents probably the native Chaldaean name of this deity, while Il is the Semitic equivalent. Il, of course, is but a variant of El, the root of the well-known Biblical Elohim as well as of the Arabic Allah. It is this name which Diodorus represents under the form of Elms ['H??oc), 7 and Sanchoniathon, or rather Philo-Byblius, under that of Elus or Ilus. The meaning of the word is simply "God," or perhaps "the god" emphatically. Ra, the Cushite equivalent, must be considered to have had the same force originally, though in Egypt it received a special application to the sun, and became the proper name of that particular deity. The word is lost in the modern Ethiopic. It formed an element in the native name of Babylon, which was Ka-ra, the Cushite equivalent of the Semitic Bab-il, an expression signifying "the gate of God."

Ra is a god with few peculiar attributes. He is a sort of fount and origin of deity, too remote from man to be much worshipped or to excite any warm interest. There is no evidence of his having had any temple in Chaldaea during the early times. A belief in his existence is implied rather than expressed in inscriptions of the primitive kings, where the Moon-god is said to be "brother's son of Ana, and eldest son of Bil, or Belus." We gather from this that Bel and Ana were considered to have a common father; and later documents sufficiently indicate that that common father was Il or Ra. We must conclude from the name Babil, that Babylon was originally under his protection, though the god specially worshipped in the great temple there seems to have been in early times Bel, and in later times Merodach. The identification of the Chaldaean, Il or Ra with Saturn, which Diodorus makes, and which may seem to derive some confirmation from Philo-Byblius, is certainly incorrect, so far as the planet Saturn, which Diodorus especially mentions, is concerned; but it may be regarded as having a basis of truth, inasmuch as Saturn was in one sense the chief of the gods, and was the father of Jupiter and Pluto, as Ra was of Bil and Ana.

ANA.

Ana, like Il and Ra, is thought to have been a word originally signifying "God," in the highest sense. The root occurs probably in the Annedotus and Oannes of Berosus, as well as in Philo-Byblius's Anobret. In its origin it is probably Cushite: but it was adopted by the Assyrians, who inflected the word which was indeclinable in the Chaldaean tongue, making the nominative Anu, the genitive Ani, and the accusative Ana.

Ana is the head of the first Triad, which follows immediately after the obscure god Ra. His position is well marked by Damascius, who gives the three gods, Anus, Illinus, and Aus, as next in succession to the primeval pair, Assorus and Missara. He corresponds in many respects to the classical Hades or Pluto, who, like him, heads the triad to which he belongs. His epithets are chiefly such as mark priority and antiquity. He is called "the old Ana," "the original chief," perhaps in one place "the father of the gods," and also "the Lord of spirits and demons." Again, he bears a number of titles which serve to connect him with the infernal regions. He is "the king of the lower world," the "Lord of darkness" or "death," "the ruler of the far-off city," and the like. The chief seat of his worship is Huruk or Erech—the modern Warka—which becomes the favorite Chaldaean burying city, as being under his protection. There are some grounds for thinking that one of his names was Dis. If this was indeed so, it would seem to follow, almost beyond a doubt, that Dis, the lord of Orcus in Roman mythology, must have been a reminiscence brought from the East—a lingering recollection of Dis or Ana, patron god of Erech (Opex of the LXX), the great city of the dead, the necropolis of Lower Babylonia. Further, curiously enough, we have, in connection with this god, an illustration of the classical confusion between Pluto and Plutus; for Ana is "the layer-up of treasures"—the "lord of the earth" and of the "mountains," whence the precious metals are derived.

The worship of Ana by the kings of the Chaldaean series is certain. Not only did Shanias-vul, the son of Ismi-dagon, raise a temple to the honor of Ana and his son Vul at Kileh-Shergat (or Asshur) about B.C. 1830— whence that city appears in later times to have borne the name of Telane, or "the mound of Ana"—but Urukh himself mentions him as a god in an inscription quoted above; and there is reason to believe that from at least as early a date he was recognized as the presiding deity at Erech or Warka. This is evident from the fact, that though the worship of Beltis superseded that of Ana in the great temple at that place from a very remote epoch, yet the temple itself always retained the title of Bit-Ana (or Beth-Ana), "the house of Ana;" and Beltis herself was known commonly as "the lady of Bit-Ana," from the previous dedication to this god of the shrine in question. Ana must also have been worshipped tolerably early at Nipur (Rifer), or that city could scarcely have acquired, by the time of Moses, the appellation of Calneh in the Septuagint translation, which is clearly Kal Ana, "the fort of Ana."

Ana was supposed to have a wife, Anata, of whom a few words will be said below. She bore her husband a numerous progeny. One tablet shows a list of nine of their children, among which, however, no name occurs of any celebrity. But there are two sons of Ana mentioned elsewhere, who seem entitled to notice. One is the god of the atmosphere, Vul (?), of whom a full account will be hereafter given. The other bears the name of Martu, and may be identified with the Brathy of Sanchoniathon. He represents "Darkness," or "the West," corresponding to the Erebus of the Greeks.

ANATA.

Anat or Anata has no peculiar characteristics. As her name is nothing but the feminine form of the masculine Ana, so she herself is a mere reflection of her husband. All his epithets are applied to her, with a simple difference of gender. She has really no personality separate from his, resembling Amente in Egyptian mythology, who is a mere feminine Ammon. She is rarely, if ever, mentioned in the historical and geographical inscriptions.

BIL, or ENU.

Bil or Enu is the second god of the first Triad. He is, probably, the Illinus (Il-Enu or "God Enu ") of Damascius. His name, which seems to mean merely "lord," is usually followed by a qualificative adjunct, possessing great interest. It is proposed to read this term as Nipru, or in the feminine Niprut, a word which cannot fail to recall the Scriptural Nimrod, who is in the Septuagint Nebroth. The term nipru seems to be formed from the root napar, which is in Syriac to "pursue," to "make to flee," and which has in Assyrian nearly the same meaning. Thus Bil-Nipru would be aptly translated as "the Hunter Lord," or "the god presiding over the chase," while, at the same time, it might combine the meaning of "the Conquering Lord" or "the Great Conqueror."

On these grounds it is reasonable to conclude that we have, in this instance, an admixture of hero-worship in the Chaldaean religion. Bil-Nipru is probably the Biblical Nimrod, the original founder of the monarchy, the "mighty hunter" and conqueror. At the same time, however, that he is this hero deified, he represents also, as the second god of the first Triad, the classical Jupiter. He is "the supreme," "the father of the gods," "the procreator," "the Lord," par excellence, "the king of all the spirits," "the lord of the world," and again, "the lord of all the countries." There is some question whether he is altogether to be identified with the Belus of the Greek writers, who in certain respects rather corresponds to Merodach. When Belus, however, is called the first king, the founder of the empire, or the builder of Babylon, it seems necessary to understand Bil-Nipru or Bel-Nimrod. Nimrod, we know, built Babylon; and Babylon was called in Assyrian times "the city of Bil-Nipru," while its famous defences—the outer and the inner wall—were known, even under Nebuchadnezzar, by the name of the same god.—Nimrod, again, was certainly the founder of the kingdom; and, therefore, if Bil-Nipru is his representative, he would be Belus under that point of view.

The chief seat of Bel-Nimrod's worship was undoubtedly Nipur (Niffer) or Calneh. Not only was this city designated by the very same name as the god, and specially dedicated to him and to his wife Beltis, but Bel-Nimrod is called "Lord of Nipra," and his wife "Lady of Nipra," in evident allusion to this city or the tract wherein it was placed. Various traditions, as will be hereafter shown, connect Nimrod with Niffer, which may fairly be regarded as his principal capital. Here then he would be naturally first worshipped upon his decease; and here seems to have been situated his famous temple called Kharris-Nipra, so noted for its wealth, splendor, and antiquity, which was an object of intense veneration to the Assyrian kings. Besides this celebrated shrine, he does not appear to have possessed many others. He is sometimes said to have had four "arks" or "tabernacles;" but the only places besides Niffer, where we know that he had buildings dedicated to him, are Calah (Nimrud) and Dur-Kurri-galzu (Akkerkuf). At the same time he is a god almost universally acknowledged in the invocations of the Babylonian and Assyrian kings, in which he has a most conspicuous place. In Assyria he seems to be inferior only to Asshur; in Chaldaea to Ra and Ana.

Of Beltis, the wife of Bel-Nimrod, a full account will be given presently. Nin or Ninip—the Assyrian Hercules—was universally regarded as their son; and he is frequently joined with Bel-Nimrod in the invocations. Another famous deity, the Moon-god, Sin or Hurki, is also declared to be Bel-Nimrod's son in some inscriptions. Indeed, as "the father of the gods," Bel-Nimrod might evidently claim an almost infinite paternity.

The worship of Bel-Nimrod in Chaldaea extends through the whole time of the monarchy. It has been shown that he was probably the deified Nimrod, whose apotheosis would take place shortly after his decease. Urukh, the earliest monumental king, built him a temple at Niffer; and Kurri-galzu, one of the latest, paid him the same honor at Akkerkuf. Urukh also frequently mentions him in his inscriptions in connection with Hurki, the Moon-god, whom he calls his "eldest son."

BELTIS.

Beltis, the wife of Bel-Nimrod, presents a strong contrast to Anata, the wife of Ana. She is far more than the mere female power of Bel-Nimrod, being in fact a separate and very important deity. Her common title is "the Great Goddess." In Chaldaea her name was Mulita or Enuta—both words signifying "the Lady;" in Assyria she was Bilta or Bilta-Nipruta, the feminine forms of Bil and Bilu-Nipru. Her favorite title was "the Mother of the Gods," or "the Mother of the Great Gods:" whence it is tolerably clear that she was the "Dea Syria" worshipped at Hierapolis under the Arian appellation of Mabog. Though commonly represented as the wife of Bel-Nimrod, and mother of his son Nin or Ninip, she is also called "the wife of Nin," and in one place "the wife of Asshur." Her other titles are "the lady of Bit-Ana," "the lady of Nipur," "the Queen of the land" or "of the lands," "the great lady," "the goddess of war and battle," and the "queen of fecundity." She seems thus to have united the attributes of the Juno, the Ceres or Demeter, the Bellona, and even the Diana of the classical nations: for she was at once the queen of heaven, the goddess who makes the earth fertile, the goddess of war and battle, and the goddess of hunting. In these latter capacities she appears, however, to have been gradually superseded by Ishtar, who sometimes even appropriates her higher and more distinctive appellations.

The worship of Beltis was wide-spread, and her temples were very numerous. At Erech (Warka) she was worshipped on the same platform, if not even in the same building with Ana. At Calneh or Nipur (Niffer), she shared fully in her husband's honors. She had a shrine at Ur (Mugheir), another at Rubesi, and another outside the walls of Babylon. Some of these temples were very ancient, those at Warka and Niffer being built by Urukh, while that at Mugheir was either built or repaired by Ismi-dagon.

According to one record, Beltis was a daughter of Ana. It was especially as "Queen of Nipur" that she was the wife of her son Nin. Perhaps this idea grew up out of the fact that at Nipur the two were associated together in a common worship. It appears to have given rise to some of the Greek traditions with respect to Semiramis, who was made to contract an incestuous marriage with her own son Ninyas, although no explanation can at present be given of the application to Beltis of that name.

HEA, or HOA.

The third god of the first Triad was Hea, or Hoa, probably the Aus of Damascus. His appellation is perhaps best rendered into Greek by the [—] of Helladius—the name given to the mystic animal, half man, half fish, which came up from the Persian Gulf to teach astronomy and letters to the first settlers on the Euphrates and Tigris. It is perhaps contained also in the word by which Berosus designates this same creature—Oannes—which may be explained as Hoa-ana, or "the god Hoa." There are no means of strictly determining the precise meaning of the word in Babylonian; but it is perhaps allowable to connect it, provisionally, with the Arabic Hiya, which is at once life and "a serpent," since, according to the best authority, there are very strong grounds for connecting Hea or Hoa with the serpent of Scripture and the Paradisaical traditions of the tree of knowledge and the tree of life.

Hoa occupies, in the first Triad, the position which in the classical mythology is filled by Poseidon or Neptune, and in some respects he corresponds to him. He is "the lord of the earth," just as Neptune is [Greek]; he is "the king of rivers;" and he comes from the sea to teach the Babylonians; but he is never called "the lord of the sea." That title belongs to Nin or Ninip. Hoa is "the lord of the abyss," or of "the great deep," which does not seem to be the sea, but something distinct from it. His most important titles are those which invest him with the character, so prominently brought out in Oe and Oannes, of the god of science and knowledge. He is "the intelligent guide," or, according to another interpretation, "the intelligent fish," "the teacher of mankind," "the lord of understanding." One of his emblems is the "wedge" or "arrowhead," the essential element of cuneiform writing, which seems to be assigned to him as the inventor, or at least the patron of the Chaldaean alphabet. Another is the serpent which occupies so conspicuous a place among the symbols of the gods on the black stones recording benefactions, and which sometimes appears upon the cylinders. [PLATE XIX., Fig. 3.] This symbol, here as elsewhere, is emblematic of superhuman knowledge—a record of the primeval belief that the serpent was more subtle than any beast of the field. The stellar name of Hoa was Kimmut; and it is suspected that in this aspect he was identified with the constellation Draco, which is perhaps the Kimah of Scripture. Besides his chief character of "god of knowledge," Hoa is also "god of life," a capacity in which the serpent would again fitly symbolize him. He was likewise "god of glory," and "god of giving," being, as Berosus said, the great giver of good gifts to man.

The monuments do not contain much evidence of the early worship of Hoa. His name appears on a very ancient stone tablet brought from Mugheir (Ur); but otherwise his claim to be accounted one of the primeval gods must rest on the testimony of Berosus and Helladius, who represent him as known to the first settlers. He seems to have been the tutelary god of Is or Hit, which Isidore of Charax calls Aeipolis, or "Hea's city;" but there is no evidence that this was a very ancient place. The Assyrian kings built him temples at Asshur and Calah.

Hoa had a wife Dav-Kina, of whom a few words will be said presently. Their most celebrated son was Merodach or Bel-Merodach, the Belus of Babylonian times. As Kimmut, Hoa was also the father of Nebo, whose functions bear a general resemblance to his own.

DAV-KINA.

Dav-Kina, the wife of Hoa, is clearly the Dauke or Davke of Damascius who was the wife of Ails and mother of Belus (Bel-Merodach). Her name is thought to signify "the chief lady." She has no distinctive titles or important position in the Pantheon, but, like Anata, takes her husband's epithets with a mere distinction of gender.

SIN, or HURKI.

The first god of the second Triad is Sin, or Hurki, the moon-deity. It is in condescension to Greek notions that Berosus inverts the true Chaldaean order, and places the sun before the moon in his enumeration of the heavenly bodies. Chaldaean mythology gives a very decided preference to the lesser luminary, perhaps because the nights are more pleasant than the days in hot countries. With respect to the names of the god, we may observe that Sin, the Assyrian or Semitic term, is a word of quite uncertain etymology, which, however, is found applied to the moon in many Semitic languages; while Hurki, which is the Chaldaean or Hamitic name, is probably from a root cognate to the Hebrew Ur, "vigilare," whence is derived the term sometimes used to signify "an angel" Ir, "a watcher."

The titles of Hurki are usually somewhat vague. He is "the chief," "the powerful," "the lord of the spirits," "he who dwells in the great heavens;" or, hyperbolically, "the chief of the gods of heaven and earth," "the king of the gods," and even "the god of the gods." Sometimes, however, his titles are more definite and particular: as, firstly, when they belong to him in respect of his being the celestial luminary—e.g., "the bright," "the shining," "the lord of the month;" and, secondly, when they represent him as presiding over buildings and architecture, which the Chaldaeans appear to have placed under his special superintendence. In this connection he is called "the supporting architect," "the strengthener of fortifications," and, more generally, "the lord of building" (Bel-zuna). Bricks, the Chaldaean building material, were of course under his protection; and the sign which designates them is also the sign of the month over which he was considered to exert particular care. His ordinary symbol is the crescent or new moon, which is commonly represented as large, but of extreme thinness ◡ ; though

not without a certain variety in the forms ◡ ◡.

The most curious and the most purely conventional representations are a linear semicircle, ◡, and an imitation of

this semicircle formed by three straight lines [64] ◡.

The illuminated part of the moon's disk is always turned directly towards the horizon, a position but rarely seen in nature.

The chief Chaldaean temple to the moon-god was at Ur or Hur (Mugheir), a city which probably derived its name from him, and which was under his special protection. He had also shrines at Babylon and Borsippa, and likewise at Calah and Dur-Sargina (Khorsabad). Few deities appear to have been worshipped with such constancy by the Chaldaean kings. His great temple at Ur was begun by Urukh, and finished by his son Ilgi—the two most ancient of all the monarchs. Later in the series we find him in such honor that every king's name during some centuries comprise the name of the moon-god in it. On the restoration of the Chaldaean power he is again in high repute. Nebuchadnezzar mentions him with respect; and Nabonidus, the last native monarch, restores his shrine at Ur, and accumulates upon him the most high-sounding titles.

The moon-god is called, in more than one inscription, the eldest son of Bel-Ninnod. He had a wife (the moon-goddess) whose title was "the great lady," and who is frequently associated with him in the lists. She and her husband were conjointly the tutelary deities of Ur or Hur; and a particular portion of the great temple there was dedicated to her honor especially.—Her "ark" or "tabernacle," which was separate from that of her husband was probably, as well as his, deposited in this sanctuary. It bore the title of "the lesser light," while his was called, emphatically, "the light."

SAN, or SANSI.

San, or Sansi, the sun-god, was the second member of the second Triad. The main element of this name is probably connected with the root shani which is in Arabic, and perhaps in Hebrew, "bright." Hence we may perhaps compare our own word "sun" with the Chaldaean "San;" for "sun" is most likely connected etymologically with "sheen" and "shine." Shamas or Shemesh, the Semitic title of the god, is altogether separate and distinct, signifying as it does, the Ministering office of the sun, and not the brilliancy of his light. A trace of the Hamitic name appears in the well-known city Bethsain, whose appellation is declared by Eugesippus to signify "domus Solis," "the house of the sun."

The titles applied to the sun-god have not often much direct reference to his physical powers or attributes. He is called indeed, in some places, "the lord of fire," "the light of the gods," "the ruler of the day," and "he who illumines the expanse of heaven and earth." But commonly he is either spoken of in a more general way, as "the regent of all things," "the establisher of heaven and earth;" or, if special functions are assigned to him, they are connected with his supposed "motive" power, as inspiring warlike thoughts in the minds of the kings, directing and favorably influencing their expeditions; or again, as helping them to discharge any of the other active duties of royalty. San is "the supreme ruler who casts a favorable eye on expeditions," "the vanquisher of the king's enemies," "the breaker-up of opposition." He "casts his motive influence" over the monarchs, and causes them to "assemble their chariots and warriors"—he goes forth with their armies, and enables them to extend their dominions—he chases their enemies before them, causes opposition to cease, and brings them back with victory to their own countries. Besides this, he helps them to sway the sceptre of power, and to rule over their subjects with authority. It seems that, from observing the manifest agency of the material sun in stimulating all the functions of nature, the Chaldaeans came to the conclusion that the sun-god exerted a similar influence on the minds of men, and was the great motive agent in human history.

The chief seats of the sun-god's worship in Chaldaea appear to have been the two famous cities of Larsa (Ellasar?) and Sippara. The great temple of the Sun, called Bit-Parra, at the former place, was erected by Urukh, repaired by more than one of the later Chaldaean monarchs, and completely restored by Nebuchadnezzar. At Sippara, the worship of the sun-god was so predominant, that Abydenus, probably following Berosus, calls the town Heliopolis. There can be little doubt that the Adrammelech, or "Fire-king," whose worship the Sepharvites (or people of Sippara) introduced into Samaria, was this deity. Sippara is called Tsipar sha Shamas, "Sippara of the Sun," in various inscriptions, and possessed a temple of the god which was repaired and adorned by many of the ancient Chaldaean kings, as well as by Nebuchadnezzar and Nabonidus.

> The general prevalence of San's worship is indicated most clearly by the cylinders. Few comparatively of those which have any divine symbol upon them are without his. The symbol is either a simple circle ◯, a quartered disk ⊗, or a four-rayed orb of a more elaborate character ⊛.

San or Sansi had a wife, Ai, Gula, or Anunit, of whom it now follows to speak.

AI, GULA, or ANUNIT.

Ai, Gula, or Anunit, was the female power of the sun, and was commonly associated with San in temples and invocations. Her names are of uncertain signification, except the second, Gula, which undoubtedly means "great," being so translated in the vocabularies. It is suspected that the three terms may have been attached respectively to the "rising," the "culminating," and the "setting sun," since they do not appear to interchange; while the name Gula is distinctly stated in one inscription to belong to the "great" goddess, "the wife of the meridian Sun." It is perhaps an objection to this view, that the male Sun, who is decidedly the superior deity, does not appear to be manifested in Chaldaea under any such threefold representation.

As a substantive deity, distinct from her husband, Gula's characteristics are that she presides over life and over fecundity. It is not quite clear whether these offices belong to her alone, or whether she is associated in each of them with a sister goddess. There is a "Mistress of Life," who must be regarded as the special dispenser of that blessing; and there is a "Mistress of the Gods," who is expressly said to "preside over births." Concerning these two personages we cannot at present determine whether they are really distinct deities, or whether they are not rather aspects of Gula, sufficiently marked to be represented in the temples by distinct idols.

Gula was worshipped in close combination with her husband, both at Larsa and Sippara. Her name appears in the inscriptions connected with both places; and she is probably the "Anammelech," whom the Sepharvites honored in conjunction with Adrammelech, the "Fire-King." In later times she had also temples independent of her husband, at Babylon and Borsippa, as well as at Calah Asshur.

The emblem now commonly regarded as symbolizing Gula is the eight-rayed disk or orb, which frequently accompanies the orb with four rays in the Babylonian representations. In

lieu of a disk, we have sometimes an eight-rayed star ⁕,

and even occasionally a star with six rays only ✳.

It is curious that the eight-rayed star became at an early period the universal emblem of divinity: but perhaps we can only conclude from this the stellar origin of the worship generally, and not any special pre-eminence or priority of Anunit over other deities.

VUL, OR IVA

The third member of the second Triad is the god of the atmosphere, whose name it has been proposed to render phonetically in a great variety of ways. Until a general agreement shall be established, it is thought best to retain a name with which readers are familiar; and the form Vul will therefore be used in these volumes. Were Iva the correct articulation, we might regard the term as simply the old Hamitic name for "the air," and illustrate it by the Arabic heva, which has still that meaning.

The importance of Vul in the Chaldaean mythology, and his strong positive character, contrast remarkably with the weak and shadowy features of Uranus, or AEther, in the classical system. Vul indeed corresponds in great measure with the classical Zeus or Jupiter, being, like him, the real "Prince of the power of the air," the lord of the whirlwind and the tempest, and the wielder of the thunderbolt. His standard titles are "the minister of heaven and earth," "the Lord of the air," "he who makes the tempest to rage." He is regarded as the destroyer of crops, the rooter-up of trees, the scatterer of the harvest. Famine, scarcity, and even their consequence, pestilence, are assigned to him. He is said to have in his hand a "flaming sword," with which he effects his works of destruction; and this "flaming sword," which probably represents lightning, becomes his emblem upon the tablets and cylinders, where it is figured as a double or triple bolt. [PLATE XIX., Fig. 4.] Vul again, as the god of the atmosphere, gives the rain; and hence he is "the careful and beneficent chief," "the giver of abundance," "the lord of fecundity." In this capacity he is naturally chosen to preside over canals, the great fertilizers of Babylonia; and we find among his titles "the lord of canals," and "the establisher of works of irrigation."

There is not much evidence of the worship of Vul in Chaldaea during the early times. That he must have been known appears from the fact of his name forming an element in the name of Shamas-Vul, son of Ismi-dagon, who ruled over Chaldaea about B.C. 1850. It is also certain that this Shamas-Vul set up his worship at Asshur (Kileh-Sherghat) in Assyria, associating him there with his father Ana, and building to them conjointly a great temple. Further than this we have no proof that he was an object of worship in the time of the first monarchy; though in the time of Assyrian preponderance, as well as in that of the later Babylonian Empire, there were few gods more venerated.

Vul is sometimes associated with a goddess, Shala or Tala, who is probably the Salambo or Salambas of the lexicographers. The meaning of her name is uncertain; and her epithets are for the most part obscure. Her ordinary title is sacrat or sharrat, "queen," the feminine of the common word sar, which means "Chief," "King," or "Sovereign."

BAR, NIN, or NINIP.

If we are right in regarding the five gods who stand next to the Triad formed of the Moon, the Sun, and the Atmosphere, as representatives of the five planets visible to the naked eye, the god Nin, or Ninip, should be Saturn. His names, Bar and Nin, are respectively a Semitic and a Hamitic term signifying "lord" or "master." Nin-ip, his full Hamitic appellation, signifies "Nin, by name," or "he whose name is Nin;" and similarly, his full Semitic appellation seems to have been Barshem, "Bar, by name," or "he whose name is Bar"—a term which is not indeed found in the inscriptions, but which appears to have been well known to the early Syrians and Armenians, and which was probably the origin of the title Barsemii, borne by the kings of Hatra (Hadhr near Kileh-Sherghat) in Roman times.

In character and attributes the classical god whom Nin most closely resembles is, however, not Saturn, but Hercules. An indication of this connection is perhaps contained in the Herodotean genealogy, which makes Hercules an ancestor of Ninus. Many classical traditions, we must remember, identified Hercules with Saturn; and it seems certain that in the East at any rate this identification was common. So Nin, in the inscriptions, is the god of strength and courage. He is "the lord of the brave," "the champion," "the warrior who subdues foes," "he who strengthens the heart of his followers;" and again, "the destroyer of enemies," "the reducer of the disobedient," "the exterminator of rebels," "he whose sword is good." In many respects he bears a close resemblance to Nergal or Mars. Like him, he is a god of battle and of the chase, presiding over the king's expeditions, whether for war or hunting, and giving success in both alike. At the same time he has qualities which seem wholly unconnected with any that have been hitherto mentioned. He is the true "Fish-God" of Berosus, and is figured as such in the sculptures. [PLATE XIX., Fig. 5.] In this point of view he is called "the god of the sea," "he who dwells in the sea," and again, somewhat curiously, "the opener of aqueducts." Besides these epithets, he has many of a more general character, as "the powerful chief," "the supreme," "the first of the gods," "the favorite of the gods," "the chief of the spirits," and the like. Again, he has a set of epithets which seem to point to his stellar character, very difficult to reconcile with the notion that, as a celestial luminary, he was Saturn. We find him called "the light of heaven and earth," "he who, like the sun, the light of the gods, irradiates the nations." These phrases appear to point to the Moon, or to some very brilliant star, and are scarcely reconcilable with the notion that he was the dark and distant Saturn.

Nin's emblem in Assyria is the Man-bull, the impersonation of strength and power. [PLATE XIX., Fig. 6.] He guards the palaces of the Assyrian kings, who reckon him their tutelary god, and give his name to their capital city. We may conjecture that in Babylonia his emblem was the sacred fish, which is often seen under different forms upon the cylinders. [PLATE XIX., Fig. 7.]

The monuments furnish no evidence of the early worship of Nin in Chaldaea. We may perhaps gather the fact from Berosus' account of the Fish-God as an early object of veneration in that region, as well as from the Hamitic etymology of the name by which he was ordinarily known even in Assyria. There he was always one of the most important deities. His temple at Nineveh was very famous, and is noticed by Tacitus in his "Annals;" and he had likewise two temples at Calah (Nimrud), both of them buildings of some pretension.

It has been already mentioned that Nin was the son of Bel-Nimrod, and that Beltis was both his wife and his mother. These relationships are well established, since they are repeatedly asserted. One tablet, however, inverts the genealogy, and makes Bel-Nimrod the son of Nin, instead of his father. The contradiction perhaps springs from the double character of this divinity, who, as Saturn, is the father, but, as Hercules, the son of Jupiter.

BEL-MERODACH.

Bel-Merodach is, beyond all doubt, the planet Jupiter, which is still called Bel by the Mendaeans. The name Merodach is of uncertain etymology and meaning. It has been compared with the Persian Mardak, the diminutive of mard, "a man," and with the Arabic Mirrich, which is the name of the planet Mars. But, as there is every reason to believe that the term belongs to the Hamitic Babylonian, it is in vain to have recourse to Arian or Semitic tongues for its derivation. Most likely the word is a descriptive epithet, originally attached to the name Bel, in the same way as Nipru, but ultimately usurping its place and coming to be regarded as the proper name of the deity. It is doubtful whether any phonetic representative of Merodach has been found on the monuments; if so, the pronunciation should, apparently, be Amardak, whence we might derive the Amordacia of Ptolemy.

The titles and attributes of Merodach are of more than usual vagueness. In the most ancient monuments which mention him, he seems to be called "the old man of the gods," and "the judge;" he also certainly has the gates, which in early times were the seats of justice, under his special protection. Thus he would seem to be the god of justice and judgment—an idea which may have given rise to the Hebrew name of the planet Jupiter, viz. sedek, "justitia." Bel-Merodach was worshipped in the early Chaldaean kingdom, as appears from the Tel-Sifr tablets. He was probably from a very remote time the tutelary god of the city of Babylon; and hence, as that city grew into importance, the worship of Merodach became more prominent. The Assyrian monarchs always especially associate Babylon with this god; and in the later Babylonian empire he becomes by far the chief object of worship. It is his temple which Herodotus describes so elaborately, and his image, which, according to the Apocryphal Daniel, the Babylonians worshipped with so much devotion. Nebuchadnezzar calls him "the king of the heavens and the earth," "the great lord," "the senior of the gods," "the most ancient," "the supporter of sovereignty," "the layer-up of treasures," etc., and ascribes to him all his glory and success.

We have no means of determining which among the emblems of the gods is to be assigned to Bel-Merodach; nor is there any sculptured form which can be certainly attached to him. According to Diodorus, the great statue of Bel-Merodach at Babylon was a figure "standing and walking." Such a form appears more often than any other upon the cylinders of the Babylonians; and it is perhaps allowable to conjecture that it may represent this favorite deity. [PLATE XIX., Fig. 8.]

ZIR-BANIT.

Bel-Merodach has a wife, with whom he is commonly associated, called Zir-banit. She had a temple at Babylon, probably attached to her husband's, and is perhaps the Babylonian Juno (Hera) of Diodorus. The essential element of her name seems to be Zir, which is an old Hamitic root of uncertain meaning, while the accompanying banit is a descriptive epithet, which may be rendered by "genetrix." Zir-banit was probably the goddess whose worship the Babylonian settlers carried to Samaria, and who is called Succoth-benoth in Scripture.

NERGAL.

Nergal, the planet Mars, whose name was continued to a late date, under the form of Nerig in the astronomical system of the Mendaeans, is a god whose character and attributes are tolerably clear and definite. His name is evidently compounded of the two Hamitic roots nir, "a man," and gala, "great;" so that he is "the great man," or "the great hero." He is the special god of war and of hunting, more particularly of the latter. His titles are "the king of battle," "the champion of the gods," "the storm ruler," "the strong begetter," "the tutelar god of Babylonia," and "the god of the chase." He is usually coupled with Nin, who likewise presides over battles and over hunting; but while Nin is at least his equal in the former sphere, Nergal has a decided pre-eminence in the latter.

We have no distinct evidence that Nergal was worshipped in the primitive times. He is first mentioned by some of the early Assyrian kings, who regard him as their ancestor. It has, however, been conjectured that, like Bil-Nipru, he represented the deified hero, Nimrod, who may have been worshipped in different parts of Chaldaea under different titles.

The city peculiarly dedicated to Nergal was Cutha or Tiggaba, which is constantly called his city in the inscriptions. He was worshipped also at Tarbisa, near Nineveh, but in Tiggaba he was said to "live," and his shrine there was one of great celebrity. Hence "the men of Cuth," when transported to Samaria by the Assyrians, naturally enough "made Nergal their god," carrying his worship with them into their new country.

Nergal's emblem, the Man-Lion.

PLATE XX

It is probable that Nergal's symbol was the Man Lion. [PLATE XX.] Nir is sometimes used in the inscriptions in the meaning of "lion;" and the Semitic name for the god himself is "Aria"—the ordinary term for the king of beasts both in Hebrew and in Syriac. Perhaps we have here the true derivation of the Greek name for the god of war, Ares, which has long puzzled classical scholars. The lion would symbolize both the fighting and the hunting propensities of the god, for he not only engages in combats upon occasions, but often chases his prey and runs it down like a hunter. Again, if Nergal is the Man-Lion, his association in the buildings with the Man-Bull would be exactly parallel with the conjunction, which we so constantly find, between him and Nin in the inscriptions.

Nergal had a wife, called Laz, of whom, however, nothing is known beyond her name. It is uncertain which among the emblems of the gods appertains to him.

ISHTAR, or NANA.

Ishtar, or Nana, is the planetary Venus, and in general features corresponds with the classical goddess. Her name Ishtar is that by which she was known in Assyria; and the same term prevailed with slight modifications among the Semitic races generally. The Phoenician form was Astarte, the Hebrew Ashtoreth; the later Mendaean form was Ashtar. In Babylonia the goddess was known as Nana, which seems to be the Naneea of the second book of Maccabees, and the Nani of the modern Syrians. No satisfactory account can at present be given of the etymology of either name; for the proposal to connect Ishtar with the Greek (Zend starann, Sanscrit tara, English star, Latin stella), though it has great names in its favor, is not worthy of much attention.

Ishtar's aphrodisiac character, though it can scarcely be doubted, does not appear very clearly in the inscriptions. She is "the goddess who rejoices mankind," and her most common epithet is "Asurah," "the fortunate," or "the happy." But otherwise her epithets are vague and general, insomuch that she is often scarcely distinguishable from Beltis. She is called "the mistress of heaven and earth," "the great goddess," "the queen of all the gods," and again "the goddess of war and battle," "the queen of victory," "she who arranges battles," and "she who defends from attacks." She is also represented in the inscriptions of one king as the goddess of the chase.

The worship of Ishtar was wide-spread, and her shrines were numerous. She is often called "the queen of Babylon," and must certainly have had a temple in that city. She had also temples at Asshur (Kileh-Sherghat), at Arbela, and at Nineveh. It may be suspected that her symbol was the naked female form, which is not uncommon upon the cylinders. [PLATE XXI., Figs. 1, 2.] She may also be represented by the rude images in baked clay so common throughout the Mesopotamian ruins, which are generally regarded as images of Mylitta. Ishtar is sometimes coupled with Nebo in such a way as to suggest the notion that she was his wife. This, however, can hardly have been her real position in the mythology, since Nebo had, as will presently appear, another wife, Varamit, whom there is no reason to believe identical with Ishtar. It is most probable that the conjunction is casual and accidental, being due to special and temporary causes.

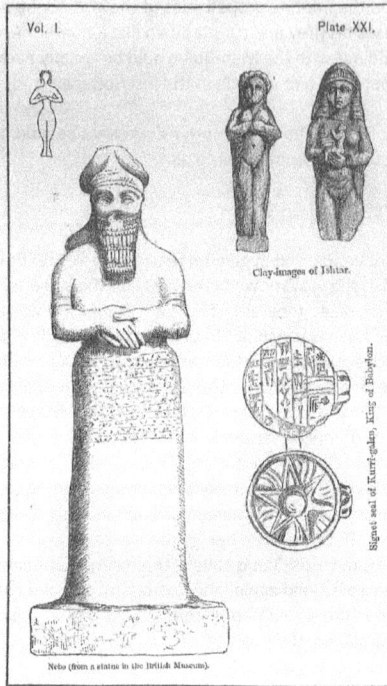

Clay-Images of Ishtar.

Signet seal of Kurri-galzu, King of Babylon.

Nebo (from a statue in the British Museum).

PLATE XXI

NEBO.

The last of the five planetary gods is Nebo, who undoubtedly represents the planet Mercury. [PLATE XXI., Fig. 3.] His name is the same, or nearly so, both in Babylonian and Assyrian; and we may perhaps assign it a Semitic derivation, from the root nibbah, "to prophesy." It is his special function to preside over knowledge and learning. He is called "the god who possesses intelligence," "he who hears from afar," "he who teaches," or "he who teaches and instructs." In this point of view, he of course approximates to Hoa, whose son he is called in some inscriptions, and to whom he bears a general resemblance. Like Hoa, he is symbolized by the simple wedge or "arrowhead," the primary and essential element of cuneiform writing, to mark his joint presidency with that God over writing and literature. At the same time Nebo has, like so many of the Chaldaean gods, a number of general titles, implying divine power, which, if they had belonged to him only, would have seemed to prove him the supreme deity. He is "the Lord of lords, who has no equal in power," "the supreme chief," "the sustainer," "the supporter," "the ever ready," "the guardian over the heavens and the earth," "the lord of the constellations," "the holder of the sceptre of power," "he who grants to kings the sceptre of royalty for the governance of their people." It is chiefly by his omission from many lists, and his humble place when he is mentioned together with the really great gods, that we know he was mythologically a deity of no very great eminence.

There is nothing to prove the early—worship of Nebo. His name does not appear as an element in any royal appellation belonging to the Chaldaean series. Nor is there any reference to him in the records of the primeval times. Still, as he is probably of Babylonian rather than Assyrian origin, and as an Assyrian king is named after him in the twelfth century B.C., we may assume that he was not unknown to the primitive people of Chaldaea, though at present their remains have furnished us with no mention of him. In later ages the chief seat of his worship was Borsippa, where the great and famous temple, known at present as the Birs-Nimrud, was dedicated to his honor. He had also a shrine at Calah (Nimrud), whence were procured the statues representing him which are now in the British Museum. He was in special favor with the kings of the great Babylonian empire, who were mostly named after him, and viewed him as presiding over their house. His symbol has not yet been recognized.

The wife of Nebo, as already observed, was Varamit or Urmit—a word which perhaps means "exalted," from the root on, "to be lifted up." No special attributes are ascribed to this goddess, who merely accompanies her husband in most of the places where he is mentioned by name.

Such, then, seem to have been the chief gods worshipped by the early Chaldaeans. It would be an endless as well as an unprofitable task to give an account of the inferior deities. Their name is "Legion;" and they are, for the most part, too vague and shadowy for effective description. A vast number are merely local; and it may be suspected that where this is the case the great gods of the Pantheon come before us repeatedly, disguised under rustic titles. We have, moreover, no clue at present to this labyrinth, on which, even with greater knowledge, it would perhaps be best for us to forbear to enter; since there is no reason to expect that we should obtain any really valuable results from its exploration.

A few words, however, may be added upon the subject of the Chaldaean cosmogony. Although the only knowledge that we possess on this point is derived from Berosus, and therefore we cannot be sure that we have really the belief of the ancient people, yet, judging from internal evidence of character, we may safely pronounce Berosus' account not only archaic, but in its groundwork and essence a primeval tradition, more ancient probably than most of the gods whom we have been considering.

"In the beginning," says this ancient legend, "all was darkness and water, and therein were generated monstrous animals of strange and peculiar forms. There were men with two wings, and some even with four, and with two faces; and others with two heads, a man's and a woman's on one body; and there were men with the heads and horns of goats, and men with hoofs like horses, and some with the upper parts of a man joined to the lower parts of a horse, like centaurs; and there were bulls with human heads, dogs with four bodies and with fishes' tails, men and horses with dogs' heads, creatures with the heads and bodies of horses, but with the tails of fish, and other animals mixing the forms of various beasts. Moreover there were monstrous fish and reptiles and serpents, and divers other creatures, which had borrowed something from each other's shapes; of all which the likenesses are still preserved in the temple of Belus. A woman ruleth them all, by name Omorka, which is in Chaldee Thalatth, and in Greek Thalassa (or "the sea"). Then Belus appeared, and split the woman in twain; and of the one half of her he made the heaven, and of the other half the earth; and the beasts that were in her he caused to perish. And he split the darkness, and divided the heaven and the earth asunder, and put the world in order; and the animals that could not bear the light perished. Belus, upon this, seeing that the earth was desolate, yet teeming with productive power, commanded one of the gods to cut off his head, and to mix the blood which flowed forth with earth, and form men therewith, and beasts that could bear the light. So man was made, and was intelligent, being a partaker of the divine wisdom. Likewise Belus made the stars, and the sun and moon, and the five planets."

It has been generally seen that this cosmogony bears a remarkable resemblance to the history of Creation contained in the opening chapters of the book of Genesis. Some have gone so far as to argue that the Mosaic account was derived from it. Others, who reject this notion, suggest that a certain "old Chaldee tradition" was "the basis of them both." If we drop out the word "Chaldee" from this statement, it may be regarded as fairly expressing the truth. The Babylonian legend embodies a primeval tradition, common to all mankind, of which an inspired author has given us the true groundwork in the first and second chapters of Genesis. What is especially remarkable is the fidelity, comparatively speaking, with which the Babylonian legend reports the facts. While the whole tone and spirit of the two accounts, and even the point of view from which they are taken, differ, the general outline of the narrative in each is nearly the same. In both we have the earth at first "without form and void," and "darkness upon the face of the deep." In both the first step taken towards creation is the separation of the mixed mass, and the formation of the heavens and the earth as the consequence of such separation. In both we have light mentioned before the creation of the sun and moon; in both we have the existence of animals before man; and in both we have a divine element infused into man at his birth, and his formation "from the dust of the ground." The only points in which the narratives can be said to be at variance are points of order. The Babylonians apparently made the formation of man and of the animals which at present inhabit the earth simultaneous, and placed the creation of the sun, moon, and planets after, instead of before, that of men and animals. In other respects the Babylonian narrative either adds to the Mosaic account, as in its description of the monsters and their destruction, or clothes in mythic language, that could never have been understood literally, the truth which in Scripture is put forth with severe simplicity. The cleaving of the woman Thalatth in twain, and the beheading of Belus, are embellishments of this latter character; they are plainly and evidently mythological; nor can we suppose them to have been at any time regarded as facts. The existence of the monsters, on the other hand, may well have been an actual belief. All men are prone to believe in such marvels; and it is quite possible, as Niebuhr supposes, that some discoveries of the remains of mammoths and other monstrous forms embedded in the crust of the earth, may have given definiteness and prominency to the Chaldaean notions on this subject.

Besides their correct notions on the subject of creation, the primitive Chaldaeans seem also to have been aware of the general destruction of mankind, on account of their wickedness, by a Flood; and of the rebellious attempt which was made soon after the Flood to concentrate themselves in one place, instead of obeying the command to "replenish the earth" an attempt which was thwarted by means of the confusion of their speech. The Chaldaean legends embodying these primitive traditions were as follows:—

"God appeared to Xisuthrus (Noah) in a dream, and warned him that on the fifteenth day of the month Daesius, mankind would be destroyed by a deluge. He bade him bury in Sippara, the City of the Sun, the extant writings, first and last; and build a ship, and enter therein with his family and his close friends; and furnish it with meat and drink; and place on board winged fowl, and four-footed beasts of the earth; and when all was ready, set sail. Xisuthrus asked 'Whither he was to sail?' and was told, 'To the gods, with a prayer that it might fare well with mankind.' Then Xisuthrus was not disobedient to the vision, but built a ship five furlongs (3125 feet) in length, and two furlongs (1250 feet) in breadth; and collected all that had been commanded him, and put his wife and children and close friends on board. The flood came; and as soon as it ceased, Xisuthrus let loose some birds, which, finding neither food nor a place where they could rest, came back to the ark. After some days he again sent out the birds, which again returned to the ark, but with feet covered with mud. Sent out a third time, the birds returned no more, and Xisuthrus knew that land had reappeared: so he removed some of the covering of the ark, and looked, and behold! the vessel had grounded on a mountain. Then Xisuthrus went forth with his wife and his daughter, and his pilot, and fell down and worshipped the earth, and built an altar, and offered sacrifice to the gods; after which he disappeared from sight, together with those who had accompanied him. They who had remained in the ark and not gone forth with Xisuthrus, now left it and searched for him, and shouted out his name; but Xisuthrus was not seen any more. Only his voice answered them out of the air, saying, 'Worship God; for because I worshipped God, am I gone to dwell with the gods; and they who were with me have shared the same honor.' And he bade them return to Babylon, and recover the writings buried at Sippara, and make them known among men; and he told them that the land in which they then were was Armenia. So they, when they had heard all, sacrificed to the gods and went their way on foot to Babylon, and, having reached it, recovered the buried writings from Sippara, and built many cities and temples, and restored Babylon. Some portion of the ark still continues in Armenia, in the Gordiaean (Kurdish) Mountains; and persons scrape off the bitumen from it to bring away, and this they use as a remedy to avert misfortunes."

"The earth was still of one language, when the primitive men, who were proud of their strength and stature, and despised the gods as their inferiors, erected a tower of vast height, in order than they might mount to heaven. And the tower was now near to heaven, when the gods (or God) caused the winds to blow and overturned the structure upon the men, and made them speak with divers tongues; wherefore the city was called Babylon."

Here again we have a harmony with Scripture of the most remarkable kind—a harmony not confined to the main facts, but reaching even to the minuter points, and one which is altogether most curious and interesting. The Babylonians have not only, in common with the great majority of nations, handed down from age to age the general tradition of the Flood, but they are acquainted with most of the particulars of the occurrence. They know of the divine warning to a single man, the direction to construct a huge ship or ark, the command to take into it a chosen few of mankind only, and to devote the chief space to "winged fowl and four-footed beasts of the earth." They are aware of the tentative sending out of birds from it, and of their returning twice, but when sent out a third time returning no more. They know of the egress from the ark by removal of some of its covering, and of the altar built and the sacrifice offered immediately afterwards. They know that the ark rested in Armenia; that those who escaped by means of it, or their descendants, journeyed towards Babylon; that there a tower was begun, but not, completed, the building being stopped by divine interposition and a miraculous confusion of tongues. As before, they are not content with the plain truth, but must amplify and embellish it. The size of the ark is exaggerated to an absurdity, and its proportions are misrepresented in such a way as to outrage all the principles of naval architecture. The translation of Xisuthrus, his wife, his daughter, and his pilot—a reminiscence possibly of the translation of Enoch—is unfitly as well as falsely introduced just after they have been miraculously saved from destruction. The story of the Tower is given with less departure from the actual truth. The building is, however, absurdly represented as an actual attempt to scale heaven; and a storm of wind is somewhat unnecessarily introduced to destroy the Tower, which from the Scripture narrative seems to have been left standing. It is also especially to be noticed that in the Chaldaean legends the whole interest is made narrow and local. The Flood appears as a circumstance in the history of Babylonia; and the priestly traditionists, who have put the legend into shape, are chiefly anxious to make the event redound to the glory of their sacred books, which they boast to have been the special objects of divine care, and represent as a legacy from the antediluvian ages. The general interests of mankind are nothing to the Chaldaean priests, who see in the story of the Tower simply a local etymology, and in the Deluge an event which made the Babylonians the sole possessors of primeval wisdom.

CHAPTER VIII

HISTORY AND CHRONOLOGY

"The beginning of his kingdom was Babel, and Erech, and Accad, and Calneh, in the land of Shinar."—
GEN. X. 10.

The establishment of a Cushite kingdom in Lower Babylonia dates probably from (at least) the twenty-fourth or twenty-fifth century before our era. Greek traditions' assigned to the city of Babylon an antiquity nearly as remote; and the native historian, Berosus, spoke of a Chaldaean dynasty as bearing rule anterior to B.C. 2250. Unfortunately the works of this great authority have been lost; and even the general outline of his chronological scheme, whereof some writers have left us an account, is to a certain extent imperfect; so that, in order to obtain a definite chronology for the early times, we are forced to have recourse, in some degree, to conjecture. Berosus declared that six dynasties had reigned in Chaldaea since the great flood of Xisuthrus, or Noah. To the first, which consisted of 86 kings, he allowed the extravagant period of 34,080 years. Evechous, the founder of the dynasty, had enjoyed the royal dignity for 2400 years, and Chomasbelus, his son and successor, had reigned 300 years longer than his father. The other 84 monarchs had filled up the remaining space of 28,980 years—their reigns thus averaging 345 years apiece. It is clear that these numbers are unhistoric; and though it would be easy to reduce them within the limits of credibility by arbitrary suppositions—as for instance, that the years of the narrative represent months or days—yet it may reasonably be doubted whether we should in this way be doing any service to the cause of historic truth. The names Evechous and Chomasbelus seem mythic rather than real; they represent personages in the Babylonian Pantheon, and can scarcely have been borne by men. It is likely that the entire series of names partook of the same character, and that, if we possessed them, their bearing would be found to be, not historic, but mythological. We may parallel this dynasty of Berosus, where he reckons king's reigns by the cyclical periods of sosses and ners, with Manetho's dynasties of Gods and Demigods in Egypt, where the sum of the years is nearly as great.

It is necessary, then, to discard as unhistorical the names and numbers assigned to his first dynasty by Berosus, and to retain from this part of his scheme nothing but the fact which he lays down of an ancient Chaldaean dynasty having ruled in Babylonia, prior to a conquest, which led to the establishment of a second dynasty, termed by him Median.

The scheme of Berosus then, setting aside his numbers for the first period, is—according to the best extant authorities, as follows:—

		Years.	B.C.	B.C.
Dynasty I. of ? Chaldæan kings		?	?	2286
" II. of 8 Median "		234	2286	2052
" III. of 11 ? "		48	2052	2004
" IV. of 49 Chaldæan "		458	2004	1546
" V. of 9 Arabian "		245	1546	1301
" VI. of 45 ? "		526	1301	775
Reign of Pul (Chaldæan king)		28	775	747
Dynasty VII. of 13 ? kings		122	747	625
" VIII. of 6⁷ Babylonian "		87	625	538

It will be observed that this table contains certain defects and weaknesses, which greatly impair its value, and prevent us from constructing upon it, without further aid, an exact scheme of chronology. Not only does a doubt attach to one or two of the numbers—to the years, i.e., of the second and third dynasty—but in two cases we have no numbers at all set down for us, and must supply them from conjecture, or from extraneous sources, before we can make the scheme available. Fortunately in the more important case, that of the seventh dynasty, the number of years can be exactly supplied without any difficulty. The Canon of Ptolemy covers, in fact, the whole interval between the reign of Pul and the close of the Babylonian Empire, giving for the period of the seventh dynasty 13 reigns in 122 years, and for that of the eighth 5 reigns in 87 years. The length of the reign of Pul can, however, only be supplied from conjecture. As it is not an unreasonable supposition that he may have reigned 28 years, and as this number harmonizes well with the chronological notices of the monuments, we shall venture to assume it, and thus complete the scheme which the fragments of Berosus imperfect.

This scheme, in which there is nothing conjectural except the length of the reign of Pul, receives very remarkable confirmation from the Assyrian monuments. These inform us, first, that there was a conquest of Babylon by a Susianian monarch 1635 yers before the capture of Susa by Asshurbanipal, the son of Esarhaddon; and, secondly, that there was a second conquest by an Assyrian monarch 600 years before the occupation of Babylon by Esarhaddon's father, Sennacherib. Now Sennacherib's occupation of Babylon was in B.C. 702; and 600 years before this brings us to B.C. 1302, within a year of the date which the scheme assigns to the accession of the seventh dynasty. Susa was taken by Asshur-bani-pal probably in B.C. 651; and 1635 years before this is B.C. 2286, or the exact year marked in the scheme for the accession of the second (Median) dynasty. This double coincidence can scarcely be accidental; and we may conclude, therefore, that we have in the above table at any rate a near approach to the scheme of Babylonian chronology as received among both the Babylonians and Assyrians in the seventh century before our era.

Whether the chronology is wholly trustworthy is another question. The evidence both of the classical writers and of the monuments is to the effect that exact chronology was a subject to which the Babylonians and Assyrians paid great attention. The "Canon of Ptolemy," which contained an exact Babylonian computation of time from B.C. 747 to B.C. 331, is generally allowed to be a most authentic document, and one on which we may place complete reliance. The "Assyrian Canon," which gives the years of the Assyrian monarchs from B.C. 911 to B.C. 660, appears to be equally trustworthy. How much further exact notation went back, it is impossible to say. All that we know is, first, that the later Assyrian monarchs believed they had means of fixing the exact date of events in their own history and in that of Babylon up to a time distant from their own as much as sixteen or seventeen hundred years; and secondly, that the chronology which result from their statements and those of Berosus is moderate, probably, and in harmony with all the knowledge which we obtain of the East from other sources. It is proposed therefore, in the present volumes, to accept the general scheme of Berosus as, in all probability, not seriously in error; and to arrange the Chaldaean, Assyrian, and Babylonian history on the framework which it furnishes.

Chaldaean history may therefore be regarded as opening upon us at a time anterior, at any rate by a century or two, to B.C. 2286. It was then that Nimrod, the son or descendant of Cush, set up a kingdom in Lower Mesopotamia, which attracted the attention of surrounding nations. The people, whom he led, came probably by sea; at any rate, their earliest settlements were on the coast; and Ur or Hur, on the right bank of the Euphrates, at a very short distance from its embouchure, was the primitive capital. The "mighty hunter" rapidly spread his dominion inland, subduing or expelling the various tribes by which the country was previously occupied. His kingdom extended northwards, at least as far as Babylon,—which (as well as Erech or Huruk, Accad, and Calneh) was first founded by this monarch. Further historical details of his reign are wanting; but the strength of his character and the greatness of his achievements are remarkably indicated by a variety of testimonies, which place him among the foremost men of the Old World, and guarantee him a never-ending remembrance. At least as early as the time of Moses his name had passed into a proverb. He was known as "the mighty hunter before the Lord"—an expression which had probably a double meaning, implying at once skill and bravery in the pursuit and destruction of wild beasts, and also a genius for war and success in his aggressions upon men. In his own nation he seems to have been deified, and to have continued down to the latest times one of the leading objects of worship, under the title of Bilu-Nipru or Bel-Nimrod, which may be translated "the god of the chase," or "the great hunter."

One of his capitals, Calneh, which was regarded as his special city, appears afterwards to have been known by his name (probably as being the chief seat of his worship in the early times); and this name it still retains, slightly corrupted. In the modern Niffer we may recognize the Talmudical Nopher, and the Assyrian Nipur which is Nipru, with a mere metathesis of the two final letters. The fame of Nimrod has always been rife in the country of his domination. Arab writers record a number of remarkable traditions, in which he plays a conspicuous part; and there is little doubt but that it is in honor of his apotheosis that the constellation Orion bears in Arabian astronomy the title of El Jabbar, or "the giant." Even at the present day his name lives in the mouth of the people inhabiting Chaldaea and the adjacent regions, whose memory of ancient heroes is almost confined to three—Nimrod, Solomon, and Alexander. Wherever a mound of ashes is to be seen in Babylonia or the adjoining countries, the local traditions attach to it the name of Niinrud or Nimrod; and the most striking ruins now existing in the Mesopotamian valley, whether in its upper or its lower portion, are made in this way monuments of his glory.

Of the immediate successors of Nimrod we have no account that even the most lenient criticism can view as historical. It appears that his conquest was followed rapidly by a Semitic emigration from the country—an emigration which took a northerly direction. The Assyrians withdrew from Babylonia, which they still always regarded as their parent land, and, occupying the upper or non-alluvial portion of the Mesopotamian plain, commenced the building of great cities in a tract upon the middle Tigris. The Phoenicians removed from the shores of the Persian Gulf, and, journeying towards the northwest, formed settlements upon the coast of Canaan, where they became a rich and prosperous people. The family of Abraham, and probably other Aramaean families, ascended the Euphrates, withdrawing from a yoke which was oppressive, or at any rate unpleasant. Abundant room was thus made for the Cushite immigrants, who rapidly established their preponderance over the whole of the southern region. As war ceased to be the necessary daily occupation of the newcomers, civilization and the arts of life began to appear. The reign of the "Hunter" was followed, after no long time, by that of the "Builder." A monumental king, whose name is read doubtfully as Urkham or Urukh, belongs almost certainly to this early dynasty, and may be placed next in succession, though at what interval we cannot say, to Nimrod. He is beyond question the earliest Chaldaean monarch of whom any remains have been obtained in the country. Not only are his bricks found in a lower position than any others, at the very foundations of buildings, but they are of a rude and coarse make, and the inscriptions upon them contrast most remarkably, in the simplicity of the style of writing used and in their general archaic type, with the elaborate and often complicated symbols of the later monarchs. The style of Urukh's buildings is also primitive and simple in the extreme; his bricks are of many sizes, and ill fitted together; he belongs to a time when even the baking of bricks seems to have been comparatively rare, for sometimes he employs only the sun-dried material; and he is altogether unacquainted with the use of lime mortar, for which his substitute is moist mud, or else bitumen. There can be little doubt that he stands at the head of the present series of monumental kings, another of whom probably reigned as early as B.C. 2286. As he was succeeded by a son, whose reign seems to have been of the average length, we must place his accession at least as early as B.C. 2326. Possibly it may have fallen a century earlier.

It is as a builder of gigantic works that Urukh is chiefly known to us. The basement platforms of his temples are of an enormous size; and though they cannot seriously be compared with the Egyptian pyramids, yet indicate the employment for many years of a vast amount of human labor in a very unproductive sort of industry. The Bowariyeh mound at Warka is 200 feet square, and about 100 feet high. Its cubic contents, as originally built, can have been little, if at all, under 3,000,000 feet; and above 30,000,000 of bricks must have been used in its construction. Constructions of a similar character, and not very different in their dimensions, are proved by the bricks composing them to have been raised by the same monarch at Ur, Calneh or Nipur, and Larancha or Larsa, which is perhaps Ellasar. It is evident, from the size and number of these works, that their erector had the command of a vast amount of "naked human strength," and did not scruple to employ that strength in constructions from which no material benefit was derivable, but which were probably designed chiefly to extend his own fame and perpetuate his glory. We may gather from this that he was either an oppressor of his people, like some of the Pyramid Kings in Egypt, or else a conqueror, who thus employed the numerous captives carried off in his expeditions. Perhaps the latter is the more probable supposition; for the builders of the great fabrics in Babylonia and Chaldaea do not seem to have left behind them any character of oppressiveness, such as attaches commonly to those monarchs who have ground down their own people by servile labor.

The great buildings of Urukh appear to have been all designed for temples. They are carefully placed with their angles facing the cardinal points, and are dedicated to the Sun, the Moon, to Belus (Bel-Nimrod), or to Beltis. The temple at Mugheir was built in honor of the Moon-god, Sin or Hiuki, who was the tutelary deity of the city. The Warka temple was dedicated to Beltis. At Calneh or Nipur, Urukh erected two temples, one to Beltis and one to Belus. At Larsa or Ellasar the object of his worship was the Sun-god, San or Sansi. He would thus seem to have been no special devotee of a single god, but to have divided out his favors very fairly among the chief personages of the Pantheon.

It has been observed that both the inscriptions of this king, and his architecture, are of a rude and primitive type. Still in neither case do we seem to be brought to the earliest dawn of civilization or of art. The writing of Urukh has passed out of the first or hieroglyphic stage, and entered the second or transition one, when pictures are no longer attempted, but the lines or wedges follow roughly the old outline of the objects in his architecture, again, though there is much that is rude and simple, there is also a good deal which indicates knowledge and experience. The use of the buttress is understood; and the buttress is varied according to the material. The importance of sloping the walls of buildings inwards to resist interior pressure is thoroughly recognized. Drains are introduced to carry off moisture, which must otherwise have been very destructive to buildings composed mainly, or entirely, of crude brick. It is evident that the builders whom the king employs, though they do not possess much genius, have still such a knowledge of the most important principles of their art as is only obtained gradually by a good deal of practice. Indeed, the very fact of the continued existence of their works at the distance of forty centuries is sufficient evidence that they possessed a considerable amount of architectural skill and knowledge. We are further, perhaps, justified in concluding, from the careful emplacement of Urukh's temples, that the science of astronomy was already cultivated in his reign, and was regarded as having a certain connection with religion. We have seen that the early worship of the Chaldaeans was to a great extent astral—a fact which naturally made the heavenly bodies special objects of attention. If the series of observations which Callisthenes sent to Aristotle, dating from B.C. 2234, was in reality a record, and not a mere calculation backwards of the dates at which certain celestial phenomena must have taken place, astronomical studies must have been pretty well advanced at a period not long subsequent to Urukh.

Nor must we omit to notice, if we would estimate aright the condition of Chaldaean art under this king, the indications furnished by his signet-cylinder. So far as we can judge from the representation, which is all that we possess of this relic, the drawing on the cylinder was as good and the engraving as well executed as any work of the kind, either of the Assyrian or of the later Babylonian period. Apart from the inscription this work of art has nothing about it that is rude or primitive. The elaboration of the dresses and headgear of the figures has been already noticed. It is also worthy of remark, that the principal figure sits on an ornamental throne or chair, of particularly tasteful construction, two legs of which appear to have been modelled after those of the bull or ox. We may conclude, without much danger of mistake, that in the time of the monarch who owned this seal, dresses of delicate fabric and elaborate pattern, and furniture of a recherche and elegant shape, were in use among the people over whom he exercised dominion.

The chief capital city of Urukh appears to have been Ur. He calls himself "King of Ur and Kingi Accad;" and it is at Ur that he raises his principal buildings. Ur, too, has furnished the great bulk of his inscriptions. Babylon was not yet a place of much importance, though it was probably built by Nimrod. The second city of the Empire was Huruk or Erech: other places of importance were Larsa (Ellasar?) and Nipur or Calneh.

Urukh appears to have been succeeded in the kingdom by a son, whose name it is proposed to read as Elgi or Ilgi. Of this prince our knowledge is somewhat scanty. Bricks bearing his name have been found at Ur (Mugheir) and at Tel Eid, near Erech, or Warka; and his signet-cylinder has been recovered, and is now in the British Museum. We learn from inscriptions of Nabonidus that he completed some of the buildings at Ur, which had been left unfinished by his father; while his own bricks inform us that he built or repaired two of the principal temples at Erech. On his signet-cylinder he takes the title of "King of Ur."

After the death of Ilgi, Chaldaean history is for a time a blank. It would seem, however, that while the Cushites were establishing themselves in the alluvial plain towards the mouths of the two great rivers, there was growing up a rival power, Turanian, or Ario-Turanian, in the neighboring tract at the foot of the Zagros mountain-chain. One of the most ancient, perhaps the most ancient, of all the Asiatic cities was Susa, the Elamitic capital, which formed the centre of a nationality that endured from the twenty-third century B.C. to the time of Darius Hystaspis (B.C. 520) when it sank finally under the Persians. A king of Elam, whose court was held at Susa, led, in the year B.C. 2286 (or a little earlier), an expedition against the cities of Chaldaea, succeeded in carrying all before him, ravaged the country, took the towns, plundered the temples, and bore off into his own country, as the most striking evidence of victory, the images of the deities which the Babylonians especially reverenced. This king's name, which was Kudur-Nakhunta, is thought to be the exact equivalent of one which has a world-wide celebrity, to wit, Zoroaster. Now, according to Polyhistor (who here certainly repeats Berosus), Zoroaster was the first of those eight Median kings who composed the second dynasty in Chaldaea, and occupied the throne from about B. C. 2286 to 2052. The Medes are represented by him as capturing Babylon at this time, and imposing themselves as rulers upon the country. Eight kings reigned in space of 234 (or 224) years, after which we hear no more of Medes, the sovereignty being (as it would seem) recovered by the natives. The coincidences of the conquest the date, the foreign sovereignty and the name Zoroaster, tend to identify the Median dynasty of Berosus with a period of Susianian supremacy, which the monuments show to have been established it Chaldaea at a date not long subsequent to the reigns of Urukh and Ilgi, and to have lasted for a considerable period.

There are five monarchs known to us who may be assigned to this dynasty. The first is the Kudur-Nakhunta above named, who conquered Babylonia and established his influence there, but continued to hold his court at Susa, governing his conquest probably by means of a viceroy or tributary king. Next to him, at no great interval, may be placed Kudur-Lagamer, the Chedor-laomer of Scripture, who held a similar position to Kudur-Nakhunta, reigning himself in Elam, while his vassals, Amraphel, Arioch, and Tidal (or Turgal) held the governments respectfully of Shinar (or Upper Babylonia), Ellasar (Lower Babylonia or Chaldaea), and the Goim or the nomadic races. Possessing thus an authority over the whole of the alluvial plain, and being able to collect together a formidable army, Kudur-Lagamer resolved on a expedition up the Euphrates, with the object of extending his dominion to the Mediterranean Sea and to the borders of Egypt. At first his endeavors were successful. Together with his confederate kings, he marched as far as Palestine, where he was opposed by the native princes, Bera, king of Sodom, Birsha, king of Gomorrah, Shinab, king of Admah, Shemeber, king of Zeboiim, and the king of Bela or Zoar. A great battle was fought between the two confederated armies in the vale of Siddim towards the lower end of the Dead Sea. The invaders were victorious; and for twelve years Bera and his allies were content to own themselves subjects of the Elamitic king, whom they "served" for that period. In the thirteenth year they rebelled: a general rising of the western nations seems to have taken place; and in order to maintain his conquest it was necessary for the conqueror to make a fresh effort. Once more the four eastern kings entered Syria, and, after various successes against minor powers, engaged a second time in the valley of Siddim with their old antagonists, whom they defeated with great slaughter; after which they plundered the chief cities belonging to them. It was on this occasion that Lot, the nephew of Abraham, was taken prisoner. Laden with booty of various kinds, and encumbered with a number of captives, male and female, the conquering army set out upon its march home, and had reached the neighborhood of Damascus, when it was attacked and defeated by Abraham, who with a small band ventured under cover of night to fall upon the retreating host, which he routed and pursued to some distance. The actual slaughter can scarcely have been great; but the prisoners and the booty taken had to be surrendered; the prestige of victory was lost; and the result appears to have been that the Mesopotamian monarch relinquished his projects, and, contenting himself with the fame acquired by such distant expeditions, made no further attempt to carry his empire beyond the Euphrates.

The other three kings who may be assigned to the Elamitic dynasty are a father, son, and grandson, whose names appear upon the native monuments of Chaldaea in a position which is thought to imply that they were posterior to the kings Urukh and Ilgi, but of greater antiquity than any other monarchs who have left memorials in the country. Their names are read as Sinti-shil-khak, Kudur-Mabuk, and Arid-Sin. Of Sinti-shil khak nothing is known beyond the name. Kudur-Mabuk is said in the inscriptions of his son to have "enlarged the dominions of the city of Ur;" and on his own bricks he bears the title of Apda Martu, which probably means "Conqueror of the West." We may presume therefore that he was a warlike prince, like Kudur-Nakhunta and Kudur-Lagamer; and that, like the latter of these two kings, he made war in the direction of Syria, though he may not have carried his arms so far as his great predecessor. He and his son both held their court at Ur, and, though of foreign origin, maintained the Chaldaean religion unchanged, making additions to the ancient temples, and worshipping the Chaldaean gods under the old titles.

The circumstances which brought the Elamitic dynasty to a close, and restored the Chaldaean throne to a line of native princes, and unrecorded by any historian; nor have the monuments hitherto thrown any light upon them. If we may trust the numbers of the Armenian Eusebius, the dynasty which succeeded, ab. B.C. 2052, to the Susianian (or Median), though it counted eleven kings, bore rule for the short space of forty-eight years only. This would seem to imply either a state of great internal disturbance, or a time during which viceroys, removable at pleasure and often removed, governed the country under some foreign suzerain. In either case, the third dynasty of Berosus may be said to mark a transition period between the time of foreign subjection and that of the recovery by the native Chaldaeans of complete independence.

To the fourth Berosian dynasty, which held the throne for 458 years, from about B. C. 2004 to B. C. 1546, the monuments enable us to assign some eight or ten monarchs, whose inscriptions are characterized by a general resemblance, and by a character intermediate between the extreme rudeness of the more ancient and the comparative elegance and neatness of the later legends. Of these kings one of the earliest was a certain Ismidagon, the date of whose reign we are able to fix with a near approach to exactness. Sennacherib, in a rock inscription at Bavian, relates that in his tenth year (which was B. C. 692) he recovered from Babylon certain images of the gods which had been carried thither by Merodach-iddin-akhi, King of Babylon, after his defeat of Tiglath-Pileser, King of Assyria, 418 years previously. And the same Tiglath-Pileser relates that he rebuilt a temple in Assyria, which had been taken down 60 years before, after it had lasted 641 years from its foundation by Shamas-Vul, sun of Ismi-dagon. It results from these numbers that Ismi-dagon was king as early as B.C. 1850, or, probably a little earlier.

The monuments furnish little information concerning Ismidagon beyond the evidence which they afford of the extension of this king's dominion into the upper part of the Mesopotamian valley, and especially into the country known in later times as Assyria. The fact that Shamas-Vul, the son of Ismi-dagon, built a temple at Kileh-Sherghat, implies necessarily that the Chaldaans at this time bore sway in the upper region. Shamas-Vul appears to have been, not the eldest, but the second son of the monarch, and must be viewed as ruling over Assyria in the capacity of viceroy, either for his father or his brother. Such evidence as we possess of the condition of Assyria about this period seems to show that it was weak and insignificant, administered ordinarily by Babylonian satraps or governors, whose office was one of no great rank or dignity.

In Chaldaea, Ismi-dagon was succeeded by a son, whose name is read, somewhat doubtfully, as Gunguna or Gurguna. This prince is known to us especially as the builder of the great public cemeteries which now form the most conspicuous objects among the ruins of Mugheir, and the construction of which is so remarkable. Ismi-dagon and his son must have occupied the Chaldaean throne during most of the latter half of the nineteenth century before our era-from about B.C. 1850 to B.C. 1800.

Hitherto there has been no great difficulty in determining the order of the monumental kings, from the position of their bricks in the principal Chaldaean ruins and the general character of their inscriptions. But the relative place occupied in the series by the later monarchs is rendered very doubtful by their records being scattered and unconnected, while their styles of inscription vary but slightly. It is most unfortunate that no writer has left us a list corresponding in Babylonian history with that which Manetho put on record for Egyptian; since we are thus compelled to arrange our names in an order which rests on little more than conjecture.

The monumental king who is thought to have approached the nearest to Gurguna is Naram-Sin, of whom a record has been discovered at Babylon, and who is mentioned in a late inscription as the builder, in conjunction with his father, of a temple at the city of Agana. His date is probably about B.C. 1750. The seat of his court may be conjectured to have been Babylon, which had by this time risen into metropolitan conse quence. It is evident that, as time went on, the tendency was to remove the seat of government and empire to a greater distance from the sea. The early monarchs reign at Ur (Mugheir), and leave no traces of themselves further north than Niffer. Sin-Shada holds his court at Erech (Warka), twenty-five miles above Mugheir; while Naram-Sin is connected with the still more northern city of Babylon. We shall find a similar tendency in Assyria, as it rose into power. In both cases we may regard the fact as indicative of a gradual spread of empire towards the north, and of the advance of civilization and settled government in that direction.

A king, who disputes the palm of antiquity with Naram-Sin, has left various records at Erech or Warka, which appears to have been his capital city. It is proposed to call him Sin-Shada. He constructed, or rather re-built, the upper terrace of the Bowariyeh ruin, or great temple, which Urukh raised at Warka to Beltis; and his bricks are found in the doorway of another large ruin (the Wuswas) at the same place; it is believed, however, that in this latter building they are not in situ, but have been transferred from some earlier edifice. His reign fell probably in the latter part of the 18th, century B. C.

Several monarchs of the Sin series—i.e. monarchs into whose names the word Sin, the name of the Moon-god, enters as an element—now present themselves. The most important of them has been called Zur-Sin. This king erected some buildings at Mugheir; but he is best known as the founder of the very curious town whose ruins bear at the present day the name of Abu-Shahrein. A description of the principal buildings at this site has been already given. They exhibit certain improvements on the architecture of the earlier times, and appear to have been very richly ornamented, at least in parts. At the same time they contain among their debris remarkable proofs of the small advance which had as yet been made in some of the simplest arts. Flint knives and other implements, stone hatchets, chisels, and nails, are abundant in the ruins; and though the use of metal is not unknown, it seems to have been comparatively rare. When a metal is found, it is either gold or bronze, no trace of iron (except in ornaments of the person) appearing in any of the Chaldaean remains. Zur-Sin, Rim-Sin, and three or four other monarchs of the Sin series, whose names are imperfect or uncertain, may be assigned to the period included between B.C. 1700 and B.C. 1546.

Another monarch, and the only other monumental name that we can assign to Berosus's fourth dynasty, is a certain Nur-Vul, who appears by the Chaldaean sale-tablets to have been the immediate predecessor of Rim-Sin, the last king of the Sin series. Nur-Vul has left no buildings or inscriptions; and we seem to see in the absence of all important monuments at this time a period of depression, such as commonly in the history of nations precedes and prepares the way for a new dynasty or a conquest.

The remaining monumental kings belong almost certainly to the fifth, or Arabian, dynasty of Berosus, to which he assigns the period of 245 years —from about B.C. 1546 to B.C. 1300. That the list comprises as many as fifteen names, whereas Berosus speaks of nine Arabian kings only, need not surprise us, since it is not improbable that Berosus may have omitted kings who reigned for less than a year. To arrange the fifteen monarchs in chronological order is, unfortunately, impossible. Only three of them have left monuments. The names of the others are found on linguistic and other tablets, in a connection which rarely enables us to determine anything with respect to their relative priority or posteriority. We can, however, definitely place seven names, two at the beginning and five toward the end of the series, thus leaving only eight whose position in the list is undetermined.

The series commences with a great king, named Khammurabi, who was probably the founder of the dynasty, the "Arab" chief who, taking advantage of the weakness and depression of Chaldaea under the latter monarchs of the fourth dynasty, by intrigue or conquest established his dominion over the country, and left the crown to his descendants. Khammurabi is especially remarkable as having been the first (so far as appears) of the Babylonian monarchs to conceive the notion of carrying out a system of artificial irrigation in his dominions, by means of a canal derived from one of the great rivers. The Nahar-Khammu-rabi ("River of Khabbu-rabi "),whereof he boasts in one of his inscriptions, was no doubt, as he states, "a blessing to the Babylonians"—it "changed desert plains into well-watered fields; it spread around fertility an abundance"—it brought a whole district, previously barren, into cultivation, and it set an example, which the best of the later monarchs followed, of a mode whereby the productiveness of the country might be increased to an almost inconceivable extent.

Khammu-rabi was also distinguished as a builder. He repaired the great temple of the Sun at Senkereh and constructed for himself a new palace at Kalwadha, or Chilmad, not far from the modern Baghdad. His inscriptions have been found at Babylon, at Zerghul, and at Tel-Sifr; and it is thought probable that he made Babylon his ordinary place of residence. His reign probably covered the space from about B.C. 1546 to B.C. 1520, when he left his crown to his son, Samsu-iluna. Of this monarch our notices are exceedingly scanty. We know him only from the Tel-Sifr clay tablets, several of which are dated by the years of his reign. He held the crown probably from about B.C. 1520 to B.C. 1500.

About sixty or seventy years after this we come upon a group of names, belonging almost certainly to this same dynasty, which possess a peculiar interest, inasmuch as they serve to connect the closing period of the First, or Chaldaean, with the opening portion of the Second, or Assyrian, Monarchy. A succession of five Babylonian monarchs is mentioned on an Assyrian tablet, the object of which is to record the synchronous history of the two countries. These monarchs are contemporary with independent Assyrian princes, and have relations toward them which are sometimes peaceful, sometimes warlike. Kara-in-das, the first of the five, is on terms of friendship with Asshur-bel-nisi-su, king of Assyria, and concludes with him a treaty of alliance. This treaty is renewed between his successor, Purna-puriyas, and Buzur-Asshur, the successor of Asshur-bel-nisi-su on the throne of Assyria. Not long afterwards a third Assyrian monarch, Asshur-upallit, obtains the crown, and Purna-puriyas not only continues on the old terms of amity with him, but draws the ties which unite the two royal families closer by marrying Asshur-upallit's daughter. The issue of this marriage is a prince named Kara-khar-das, who on the death of Purna-puriyas ascends the throne of Babylon. But now a revolution occurs. A certain Nazi-bugas rises in revolt, puts Kara-khar-das to death, and succeeds in making himself king. Hereupon Asshur-upallit takes up arms, invades Babylonia, defeats and kills Nazi-bugas, and places upon the throne a brother of the murdered Kara-khar-das, a younger son of Purna-puriyas, by name Kurri-galzu, or Durri-galzu. These events may be assigned with much probability to the period between B.C. 1440 and B.C. 1380.

Of the five consecutive monarchs presented to our notice in this interesting document, two are known to us by their own inscriptions. Memorials of Purna-puriyas and Kurri-galzu, very similar in their general character, have been found in various parts of Chaldala. Those of Purna-puriyas come from Senkereh the ancient Larsa, and consist of bricks, showing that he repaired the great temple of the Sun at that city which was originally built by Urukh. Kurri-galzu's memorials comprise bricks from Mugheir (Ur) and Akkerkuf, together with his signet-seal, which was found at Baghdad in the year 1800. [PLATE XXI., Fig. 4.] It also appears by an inscription of Nabonidus that he repaired a temple at the city of Agana, and left an inscription there.

But the chief fame of Kurri-galzu arises from his having been the founder of an important city. The remarkable remains at Akkerkuf, of which an account has been given in a former chapter, mark the site of a town of his erection. It is conjectured with some reason that this place is the Dur-Kurri-galzu of the later Assyrian inscriptions—a place of so much consequence in the time of Sargon that he calls it "the key of the country."

The remaining monarchs, who are on strong grounds of probability, etymological and other, assigned to this dynasty are Saga-raktiyas, the founder of a Temple of the male and female Sun at Sippara, Ammidi-kaga, Simbar-sikhu, Kharbisikhu, Ulam-puriyas, Nazi-urdas, Mili-sikhu, and Kara-kharbi. Nothing is known at present of the position which any of these monarchs held in the dynasty, or of their relationship to the kings previously mentioned, or to each other. Most of them are known to us simply from their occurrence in a biliugual list of kings, together with Khammu-rabi, Kurri-galzu, and Purna-puriyas. The list in question appears not to be chronological.

KINGS OF CHALDÆA.

Dynasty.	B.C. to B.C.	Kings.	Events, etc.
I. (Chaldæan)	. . 2286	Nimrod . . . . . * * * * * * * * Urukh . . . . . Ilgi (son). * * * *	Founds the Empire. Builds numerous temples.
II. (Elamite)	2286 2052	Kudur-Nakhunta (Zoroaster). * * * * Kudur-Lagamer . . * * * * Sinti-shil-khak. Kudur-Mabuk (son) Arid-Sin (son).	Conquers Chaldæa, B.C. 2286. { Contemporary with Ab- { raham. Makes two expe- { ditions into Syria. Wars in Syria.
III.	2052 2004	* * * * * * * *	
IV. (Chaldæan)	2004 1546	* * * * * * * * . Ismi-dagon. . . . Gurguna (son) . . * * * * Naram-Sin. * * * * Bilat**at (a queen). Sin-Shada (son). * * * * Zur-Sin. * * * * Nur-Vul. . . . . Rim-Sin	{ Reigns from about B.C. { 1850 to 1830. { His brother, Shamas-Vul, { rules in Assyria. { Reigns from about B.C. { 1586 to 1566. { Reigns from about B.C. { 1566 to 1546. .
V. (Arab)	1546 1301	Khammu-rabí . . Samsu-iluna (son). * * * * * * * * Kara-in-das. . . . Purna-puriyas . . Kara-khar-das (son) Nazi-bugas. . . . Kurri-galzu (brother of Kara-khar-das) * * * *	{ Reigns from about B.C. { 1546 to 1520. { Reigns from about B.C. { 1520 to 1500. (Contemporary with As- { shur-bel-nisi-su, ab. B.C. (1440. { Contemporary with Buz- { ur-Asshur, B.C. 1420–1400 (Contemporary with As- { shur-upallit, B.C. 1400– (1380.
	1300	* * * * * * * *	{ Chaldæa conquered by { Tiglathi-Nin.

Modern research has thus supplied us with memorials (or at any rate with the names) of some thirty kings, who ruled in the country properly termed Chaldaea at a very remote date. Their antiquity is evidenced by the character of their buildings and of their inscriptions, which are unmistakably rude and archaic. It is further indicated by the fact that they are the builders of certainly the most ancient edifices whereof the country contains any trace. The probable connection of two of them with the only king known previously from good authority to have reigned in the country during the primitive ages confirms the conclusion drawn from the appearance of the remains themselves; which is further strengthened by the monumental dates assigned to two of them, which place them respectively in the twenty-third and the nineteenth century before our era. That the kings belong to one series, and (speaking broadly) to one time, is evidenced by the similarity of the titles which they use, by their uninterrupted worship of the same gods, and by the general resemblance of the language and mode of writing which they employ. That the time to which they belong is anterior to the rise of Assyria to greatness appears from the synchronism of the later monarchs of the Chaldaean with the earliest of the Assyrian list, as well as from the fact that the names borne by the Babylonian kings after Assyria became the leading power in the country are not only different, but of a different type. If it be objected that the number of thirty kings is insufficient for the space over which they have in our scheme been spread, we may answer that it has never been, supposed by any one that the twenty-nine or thirty kings, of whom distinct mention has been made in the foregoing account, are a complete list of all the Chaldaean sovereigns. On the contrary, it is plain that they are a very incomplete list, like that which Herodotus gives of the kings of Egypt, or that which the later Romans possessed of their early monarchs. The monuments themselves present indications of several other names of kings, belonging evidently to the same series, which are too obscure or too illegible for transliteration. And there may, of course, have been many others of whom no traces remain, or of whom none have been as yet found. On the other hand, it may be observed, that the number of the early Chaldaean kings reported by Polyhistor is preposterous. If sixty-eight consecutive monarchs held the Chaldaean throne between B.C. 2286 and B.C. 1546, they must have reigned on an average, less than eleven years apiece. Nay, if forty-nine ruled between B.C. 2004 and B.C. 1546, covering a space of little more than four centuries and a half—which is what Berosus is made to assert—these later monarchs cannot even have reigned so long as ten years each, an average which may be pronounced quite impossible in a settled monarchy such as the Chaldaean. The probability would seem to be that Berosus has been misreported, his numbers having suffered corruption during their passage through so many hands, and being in this instance quite untrustworthy. We may conjecture that the actual number of reigns which he intended to allow his fourth dynasty was nineteen, or at the utmost twenty-nine, the former of which numbers would give the common average of twenty-four years, while the latter would produce the less usual but still possible one of sixteen years.

The monarchy which we have had under review is one, no doubt, rather curious from its antiquity than illustrious from its great names, or admirable for the extent of its dominions. Less ancient than the Egyptian, it claims the advantage of priority over every empire or kingdom which has grown up upon the soil of Asia. The Arian, Turanian, and even the Semitic tribes, appear to have been in the nomadic condition, when the Cushite settlers in Lower Babylonia betook themselves to agriculture, erected temples, built cities, and established a strong and settled government. The leaven which was to spread by degrees through the Asiatic peoples was first deposited on the shores of the Persian Gulf at the mouth of the Great River; and hence civilization, science, letters, art, extended themselves northward, and eastward, and westward. Assyria, Media, Semitic Babylonia, Persia, as they derived from Chaldaea the character of their writing, so were they indebted to the same country for their general notions of government and administration, for their architecture, their decorative art, and still more for their science and literature. Each people no doubt modified in some measure the boon received, adding more or less of its own to the common inheritance. But Chaldaea stands forth as the great parent and original inventress of Asiatic civilization, without any rival that can reasonably dispute her claims. The great men of the Empire are Nimrod, Urukh, and Che-dor-laomer. Nimrod, the founder, has the testimony of Scripture that he was "a mighty one in the earth;" "a mighty hunter;" the establisher of a "kingdom," when kingdoms had scarcely begun to be known; the builder of four great and famous cities,

"Babel, and Erech, and Accad, and Calneh, in the land of Shinar," or Mesopotamia. To him belong the merit of selecting a site peculiarly fitted for the development of a great power in the early ages of the world, and of binding men together into a community which events proved to possess within it the elements of prosperity and permanence. Whether he had, indeed, the rebellious and apostate character which numerous traditions, Jewish, Arabian, and Armenian, assign to him; whether he was in reality concerned in the building of the tower related in the eleventh chapter of the Book of Genesis, we have no means of positively determining. The language of Scripture with regard to Nimrod is laudatory rather than the contrary; and it would seem to have been from a misapprehension of the nexus of the Mosaic narrative that the traditions above mentioned originated. Nimrod, "the mighty hunter before the Lord," had not in the days of Moses that ill reputation which attached to him in later ages, when he was regarded as the great Titan or Giant, who made war upon the gods, and who was at once the builder of the tower, and the persecutor who forced Abraham to quit his original country. It is at least doubtful whether we ought to allow any weight at all to the additions and embellishments with which later writers, so much wiser than Moses, have overlaid the simplicity of his narrative.

Urukh, whose fame may possibly have reached the Romans, was the great Chaldaean architect. To him belongs, apparently, the conception of the Babylonian temple, with its rectangular base, carefully placed so as to present its angles to the four cardinal points, its receding stages, its buttresses, its drains, its sloped walls, its external staircases for ascent, and its ornamental shrine crowning the whole. At any rate, if he was not the first to conceive and erect such structures, he set the example of building them on such a scale and with such solidity as to secure their long continuance, and render them well-nigh imperishable. There is no appearance in all Chaldaea, so far as it has been explored, of any building which can be even probably assigned to a date anterior to Urukh. The attempted tower was no doubt earlier; and it may have been a building of the same type, but there is no reason to believe that any remnant, or indeed any trace, of this primitive edifice, has continued to exist to our day. The structures of the most archaic character throughout Chaldaea are, one and all, the work of King Urukh, who was not content to adorn his metropolitan city only with one of the new edifices, but added a similar ornament to each of the great cities within his empire.

The great builder was followed shortly by the great conqueror. Kudur-Lagamer, the Elamitic prince, who, more than twenty centuries before our era, having extended his dominion over Babylonia and the adjoining regions, marched an army a distance of 1200 miles from the shores of the Persian Gulf to the Dead Sea, and held Palestine and Syria in subjection for twelve years, thus effecting conquests which were not again made from the same quarter till the time of Nebuchadnezzar, fifteen or sixteen hundred years afterward, has a good claim to be regarded as one of the most remarkable personages in the world's history-being, as he is, the forerunner and proto-type of all those great Oriental conquerors who from time to time have built up vast empires in Asia out of heterogeneous materials, which have in a longer or a shorter space successively crumbled to decay. At a time when the kings of Egypt had never ventured beyond their borders, unless it were for a foray in Ethiopia, and when in Asia no monarch had held dominion over more than a few petty tribes, and a few hundred miles of territory, he conceived the magnificent notion of binding into one the manifold nations inhabiting the vast tract which lies between the Zagros mountain-range and the Mediterranean. Lord by inheritance (as we may presume) of Eliun and Chaldaea or Babylonia, he was not content with these ample tracts, but, coveting more, proceeded boldly on a career of conquest up the Euphrates valley, and through Syria, into Palestine. Successful here, he governed for twelve years dominions extending near a thousand miles from east to west, and from north to south probably not much short of five hundred. It was true that he was not able to hold this large extent of territory; but the attempt and the success temporarily attending it are memorable circumstances, and were probably long held in remembrance through Western Asia, where they served as a stimulus and incentive to the ambition of later monarchs.

These, then, are the great men of the Chaldaean empire. Its extent, as we have seen, varied greatly at different periods. Under the kings of the first dynasty—to which Urukh and Ilgi belonged—it was probably confined to the alluvium, which seems then to have been not more than 300 miles in length along the course of the rivers, and which is about 70 or 80 miles in breadth from the Tigris to the Arabian desert. In the course of the second dynasty it received a vast increase, being carried in one direction to the Elamitic mountains, and in another to the Mediterranean, by the conquest of Kudur-Nakhunta and Chedor-laomer. On the defeat of the latter prince it again contracted, though to what extent we have no means of determining. It is probable that Elam or Susiana, and not unlikely that the Euphrates valley, for a considerable distance above Hit, formed parts of the Chaldaean Empire after the loss of Syria and Palestine. Assyria occupied a similar position, at any rate from the time of Ismi-dagon, whose son built a temple at Kileh-Sherghat or Asshur. There is reason to think that the subjection of Assyria continued to the very end of the dynasty, and that this region, whose capital was at Kileh-Sherghat, was administered by viceroys deriving their authority from Chaldaean monarchs. These monarchs, as has been observed, gradually removed their capital more and more northwards; by which it would appear as if their empire tended to progress in that direction.

The different dynasties which ruled in Chaldaea prior to the establishment of Assyrian influence, whether Chaldaean, Susianian, or Arabian, seem to have been of kindred race; and, whether they established themselves by conquest, or in a more peaceful manner, to have made little, if any, change in the language, religion, or customs of the Empire. The so-called Arab kings, if they are really (as we have supposed), Khammurabi and his successors, show themselves by their names and their inscriptions to be as thoroughly proto-Chaldaaan as Urukh or Ilgi. But with the commencement of the Assyrian period the case is altered. From the time of Tiglathi-Nin (about B.C. 1300), the Assyrian conqueror who effected the subjugation of Babylon, a strong Semitizing influence made itself felt in the lower country—the monarchs cease to have Turanian or Cushite and bear instead thoroughly Assyrian names; inscriptions, when they occur, are in the Assyrian language and character. The entire people seems by degrees to have been Assyrianized, or at any rate Semitized-assimilated, that is, to the stock of nations to which the Jews, the northern Arabs, the Aramaeans or Syrians, the Phoenicians, and the Assyrians belong. Their language fell into disuse, and grew to be a learned tongue studied by the priests and the literati; their Cushite character was lost, and they became, as a people, scarcely distinguishable from the Assyrians. After six centuries and a half of submission and insignificance, the Chaldaeans, however, began to revive and recover themselves—they renewed the struggle for national independence, and in the year B.C. 625 succeeded in establishing a second kingdom, which will be treated of in a later volume as the fourth or Babylonian Monarchy. Even when this monarchy met its death at the hands of Cyrus the Great, the nationality of the Chaldaeans was not swept away. We find them recognized under the Persians, and even under the Parthians, as a distinct people. When at last they cease to have a separate national existence, their name remains; and it is in memory of the successful cultivation of their favorite science by the people of Nimrod from his time to that of Alexander, that the professors of astronomical and astrological learning under the Roman Emperors receive, from the poets and historians of the time, the appellation of "Chaldaeans."